DEKE RIVERS

The Nashville Rebel

STRATTON
—PRESS—
Publishing Life

THE NASHVILLE REBEL
Copyright © 2020 **Deke Rivers**

Stratton Press Publishing
831 N Tatnall Street Suite M #188,
Wilmington, DE 19801
www.stratton-press.com
1-888-323-7009

ISBN (Paperback): 978-1-64345-687-4
ISBN (Ebook): 978-1-64345-938-7

Printed in the United States of America

Books by Same Author

The Singer and his Songs
John English, The Last of the British Invasion
The Invisible Invasion—The Unknown Force
The Taipan—The Professional
The Quest for the Three Keys
The New England Seduction
The Redemption
The Baffin Island Conspiracy
The Architect
The Stockman – Beyond the Wild Frontier
The Royal Conspiracy
The Tracks of the Caribou Trail
Media Magic
Knife or Death
April in Paris
The Scarlett Saga 1 – David Scarlett
The Scarlett Saga 2 – Richard Scarlett
The Outcast
The Fashion Designer
The Legendary Lost Treasures of King Solomon
Lobo, The Coyote Kid
The Norsemen's Myth
Lord Cromwell's Daughter
Krystal Alycia Lord

Contents

Prologue

Politics in America

Once, the American Way of Life was the envy of the World. Everyone wanted to come to America.

Then the so-called United States sent that idiot Eisenhower to Europe as "the Supreme Commander" to destroy Europe, and he certainly did that, that is for sure. Yes, in his ignorance of European Foreign Affairs, he destroyed Europe and created the USSR by handing all the smaller European Countries to Stalin, who the free World would realize, was a far greater threat than Hitler had ever been. What Hitler had attempted to do, and for which millions of German and Allied soldiers died for, the Allied Leaders just handed all Eastern Europe Countries to Stalin, virtually on a Platter! so he could create the Iron Curtain Countries or the World's largest Concentration Camp, yes, the USSR, where everyone had to learn the Russian Language as their own Languages and their own

Cultures were all **banned,** and trying to leave the now new Countries, was not an option.

The KGB made sure of that.

Yes, the Allied Leaders had screwed up, big time! Yet they all returned home as "Heroes" What? Especially Eisenhower, "the Hero," for destroying Europe? For leaving behind all the thousands of DPs (the displaced people) with nothing, to somehow survive, having lost everything!

Did Eisenhower care? Of course not! He was the "Hero!"

Why in hell, and in God's name, once Hitler had been defeated, weren't the Countries that were taken over by Hitler just returned to the original people to allow them to re-establish their original boundaries and to allow them to go back to the Pre-War conditions and their respective lives, to be able to speak their own languages and to maintain their own culture? Germany, after occupation, at least, had allowed that! But not the barbaric Stalin and his feared Red Army!

That would have been the logical solution, and that was what everyone had expected from the Allied Leaders.

Instead the incompetent Allied Leaders, led by Eisenhower and De Gaulle, turned the smaller European Counties over to Stalin? Why? Why?

Then Eisenhower and his ignorant Allied Leaders, in their misguided wisdom, created the Cold War.

Then unexpectedly, suddenly there was the Closure of the Access Road to Berlin by Stalin, and the subsequent Berlin Air Lift!

Next, Stalin created and built the infamous Berlin Wall. Oh yes, Stalin was our Allie!

Just for trivia's sake and interest, when Stalin finally passed away, **three million men** were released from the Stalin Siberian Gulags (the Soviet Siberian prison camps). How many were actually killed in these camps, we will never know! Talk about corruption. Yes, our Allie!

In addition, in his ignorance of European Affairs, Eisenhower released and set free all the Mafia-type criminals that Mussolini had so meticulously rounded up when he was in power in Italy. He had them all placed in the Sicilian jails awaiting their trials.

What did Eisenhower do?

He sent the Allied Armies into Sicily, and there he released all the Mafia-type criminals in the Italian jails and allowed them all to go free and consequently saturating the World, and specifically the so-called United States.

Yes, Eisenhower, "the Hero," was a real "Genius!" Yes, he was responsible for the creation of the worldwide Mafia as well. So much for the American knowledge of Foreign Affairs.

Well, over the years, Democracy had slowly evaporated and left the shores of America as the Politicians, Super Rich, and influential Corporations, and let's not forget the Mafia and their key People, took over the country. Together, they had introduced Corruption into the Country like never before.

Now in reality, it really depended of how much money One had, and secondly, who were your close and influential Friends in the One Percent, or Partners in Crime, yes, influential "Friends" who financially could keep you safe.

Looking forward, regretfully America had changed as the Bush-and-Cheney combination, looked after themselves, the Super Rich, their friends, and destroyed the American Middle Class in the famous Bush Crash, and thrust the country into illegal Wars based on outright lies, specifically for their own benefits—Oil!

Oh yes, and Bush selling Democracy to the Middle East when it didn't even exist in the United States of America, was a Joke! Yes, that took real brains!

Yes, the America of Old, that everyone had once envied, was now gone!

America had always called itself the United States, but the real fact was, they have never ever been United. The Country of America had its own Laws, defined as Federal Law, and then each and every one of the fifty States has its own separate State Laws. So in effect, there is no Uniform Law in Country of America. The United States is a fallacy—it does not exist.

Now it all comes down to how much money One has and Who you know.

As there is no Law as such, the Rich and influential People can do anything they want, and the others just have to learn to exist.

Just look at what happened to the USSR—the Union of Socialist Republics. When the Countries' Leaders had skimmed all the wealth for themselves and allowed the Law of the Land to become totally complacent, it all fell apart!

America, today has now more Inmates per Capita than any other Country in the World. The only difference is that we don't call our Correctional Institutions, Gulags. Yes, this is the Country that everyone envied—but not anymore!

Interesting, isn't it?

The Mafia

When Benito Mussolini came into power in Italy, He was on a mission to eliminate the Power of the Mafia, so He rounded up all the Mafia Leaders and all their Members and put them all in jail in Sicily, to await their court cases and trials and their jail sentences. It looked for a while that Italy had finally put the Mafia out of commission and rid the country from the fear, the corruption, and the perpetual violence generated by the Mafioso over the generations.

Regretfully, as Fate would have it, she, Fate, made one of her mistakes. She sent the Allied Armies into Sicily to open up another front against the Germans, but true to the incompetence of the Allied Leaders who really knew nothing about the numerous European Countries they were now entering, the Allied Leaders, led by that incomparable and clueless "Hero," Eisenhower, without having a clue to reality, released—yes, released—all the criminals from the Sicilian jails.

Subsequently, the majority of the released Mafia Leaders and all their Associates, immediately scattered around the World to start their reigns of corruption and violence all over again in their new adopted Countries. The main Target was, of course, the wonderful and accommodating and clueless United States. That incompetent so-called Leader, Eisenhower, and the other Allied Leaders had no idea what they had done!

These were the men, who created the Mob, the Underworld of Gangsters in New York City, Chicago, Las Vegas, Miami, and so on in the United States and in Montreal and Toronto in Canada. Yes, Lucky Luciano, John Gotti, Al Capone, Frank Costello, Carlo Gambino, Joseph "Bananas" Bonanno and others. Yes, they all originated from Italy and flourished in the United States and the self-proclaimed Hero, Eisenhower didn't have a clue.

So unofficially the Mafia Dons, Leaders, and Associates all thanked the hapless Allied Leaders, specifically the incompetent Eisenhower and his incompetent "Boys' Club" for releasing them all.

That is why the Mafia still exists Today and why they are still so powerful all around the World, but specifically in the United States.

Also, note that it really was the incompetent Leaders, led by Eisenhower, who actually created the USSR, when they turned over half of Europe to Stalin.

The so-called Cold War was also a creation of the hapless Allied Leaders, again specifically Eisenhower, "the Supreme Leader" who is credited for destroying the old Europe!

The Music and Entertainment Industry

Let's face it, folks, life is all about being there at the right place and at the right time, especially in the Music and Entertainment Industry. Being unique in some way that separates you from others also helps in the final scenario.

As we all can appreciate, there are many Singers, Songwriters, Composers, and Entertainers out there, trying to get a break in their Industry, and not having had that break yet, but still searching for it. Having the ability to write beautiful, appealing songs, being able to play a specific instrument, and having that magnetic charisma on stage that the audience just could not get enough of, are really things that every anxious, and very often very talented youngsters, have to contend with. They have it, or they don't.

Going back in history a little, to the time of vaudeville, with the likes of Al Jolson and Eddie Cantor. They too had the ambition, and they dared to do things differently. Yes, they both had distinctive voices and styles, but it was their stage appeal and their prancing on the stage that had the audiences coming back for more. Yes, they were being entertained visually as well and not just vocally.

Then came the big band era of Glenn Miller, Tommy and Jimmy Dorsey. Benny Goodman, Harry James, Les Brown, Stan Kenton. Louis Armstrong, Ray Anthony, and others with their string of singers—not entertainers but singers, like Doris Day, Frank Sinatra, Perry Como, Eddie Fisher, Dinah Shore and a string of others that really only complemented the bands that they sang for. The Entertainment aspect was lost! But that music was for the **Adults**, not teenagers! On stage, they stood still and sang their songs, that was all. Once again it was strictly vocal presentation. There was nothing to watch, nothing to excite, the audience. Close your eyes and listen to the music. There was no visual entertainment anymore. A record player in the middle of a dance floor was all that was needed. Yes, the audio was there, but the visual entertained was left behind.

Al Jolson had passed away.

But suddenly the fifties, the era of the Baby Boomers, changed everything!

First, there was Bill Haley & His Comets.

Then Elvis Presley, the Wild Southern Boy, "the Hillbilly Cat," "Elvis the Pelvis," hit the scene and changed the music industry forever. Suddenly it was the Teenagers, the Baby Boomers, that demanded their own music, and Elvis started the ball rolling.

Then came the fifties' rockers: Jerry Lee Lewis, Little Richard, Chuck Berry, Fats Domino, Ricky Nelson, Charlie Gracie, Larry Williams, Eddie Cochran, Buddy Holly, and the Crickets, The Platters, Brenda Lee, and so on.

Suddenly, the Teenagers changed everything. Their Music ruled the airways. Their clothing, shoes, haircuts—Everything changed.

The Victorian era had seen its last days!

"Father knows best" no longer applied.

This story takes in the World of Corruption, Politics, and Music as they all crash together in the middle of America. There is no reference to the so-called United States of America as technically they were not United and realistically have never been United!

Part 1

The Rise of the Phoenix

Chapter 1

The Baldwin Family of Kentucky

The Taurus Corporation

The Baldwin Family's History actually went back many generations back to Italy in Europe and specifically in Sicily. Yes, the family was Mafioso and had been for generations. The Godfather at that stage back in the forties in Sicily was Benito Angelina, and his son, Alberto Angelina was his Underboss, and their Consiglieri, their cousin, Luigi Rinaldi.

As the war in Europe progressed, the misguided and misinformed Allied Leaders and Allied Armies raced into Sicily and unknowingly and being totally clueless, released all the Mafia Criminals from the Sicilian jails, that Benito Mussolini had so meticulously apprehended while he was in power.

As soon as all the Mafiosi types were released, the majority of them, immediately disappeared out of Europe and scattered around the world to find new havens for themselves to exploit, and the United States of Americas was the Prime Destination, starting in New York! Yes, the presence of the Mafia in the United States and in fact all around the world can be attributed to that idiot, the Allied Supreme Leader, Dwight Eisenhower for his total incompetence and his lack of understanding of European and obviously, the World's Foreign Affairs, and specifically Italy's.

Foreign Affairs? An interesting Concept, but what was that? No idea!

Thus, the laughing Mafioso types disappeared from Europe. Some, however, remained behind to pick up the pieces and to reorganize their operations once more, once the Allied Armies had left!

Once in the United States, Alberto Louis Angelini quickly changed his name to Albert Baldwin to blend in with the American Society. Albert was on the ball as he quickly realized that New York was totally infested with all ex-Mafia Types, who were in a power struggle to gain control of the New York City Realm. The same problem existed in Chicago, so he headed south to find another town where he would blend in with the locals and where he could set up a separate arm of the Mafia. That city was Miami in Florida. Yes, he would always stay connected to the local Don in New York, with whoever was in control, as he also knew they would always have additional resources and assistance if he ever needed them.

He also set up selected operations through-out the South in smaller centers like Lexington in Kentucky, and Memphis in Tennessee, but his center of operations was Miami in Florida. Between Lexington, in Kentucky and Miami, he also set up centers in Atlanta, Georgia, Birmingham, Alabama, and New Orleans, Louisiana. There he recruited local Italians who were familiar with the "old country "ways and the rewards for belonging to the Mafia. Soon he had all the help he needed, and skillfully he made roadways into the local Police Forces in the area and the local Politicians, who were quite anxious for their support. Soon new "Clubs" opened up in all the larger cities in Kentucky and Tennessee, like Nashville, Louisville, Knoxville, Memphis, and of course his own Family Home based in the smaller center of Lexington, Kentucky

There he met and married a local beauty queen, Julie Ann Mobley. The American dream had been achieved. Over the next few years, Julie gave birth to two boys, Dwayne Angelo Baldwin, and several years later, Wayne Gino Baldwin.

As soon as the two sons turned sixteen, they became part of the Family Operations and were trained accordingly—Dwayne, specifically, in the Baldwin day-to-day Operations and Wayne in the academic arena, specifically Accounting and the money end of the Operations.

At twenty-one both were married—Dwayne to his first wife, Olivia, a very attractive would-be movie star, blonde, who Dwayne killed, on a trip down in Australia, and that was another story in itself.

Then he married Alice, a big-busted submissive hooker who obviously looked after Dwayne the way he wanted to be looked after. They had no children, nor did they want any. Dwayne couldn't wait to take over the operations from his father, Alberto, the Don. So as Alberto was getting on, slowly he started transferring some of his responsibilities over to Dwayne. Dwayne loved it.

Dwayne was ruthless, cruel, unforgiving, and he cared for no one, only himself. Alice, his vivacious wife, he knew he could replace her at any time if she could no longer satisfy his needs. Yes, she had no personality, only a vivacious body. Yes, she was replaceable as well.

Wayne, Dwayne's younger brother, on the other hand, was a quiet individual and had no grandiose aspirations at all. He found a quiet young lady, his teenage girlfriend, Jennifer Olsen, and got married. They had a son, whom they named Eric Scott Baldwin, and they lived a quiet peaceful life away from the family operations, which had been taken over by Dwayne when Alberto passed away.

Wayne was the Taurus Corporation's Accountant, so he saw the Corruption going into high gear as more and more Politicians, Policemen, Judges, and Prosecutors were being paid off for the Family Favors.

Wayne's choice of employment had been dictated to him by Alberto, his Father, years ago, who had sent him to all the applicable Colleges and Universities to get the best education for his position as Chief Accountant for the Taurus Corporation so that he could find all the applicable loopholes in the legal systems.

Chapter 2

Eric Baldwin - The Nashville Rebel

The Baldwin Family, Jessie, Wayne, and their son, Eric, lived just south of Lexington in the small community of Valley View. Wayne worked as the Chief Accountant for the Taurus Corporation in Lexington with his older brother, Dwayne, doing what, Jessie and Eric didn't know and were never told, supposedly keep the Corporation's Books straight. Whatever he was doing, they were well compensated and were living a respectable, comfortable life.

Eric was a typical teenager at the time, and enjoyed his life in school. He was in the school band, where he learnt how to play the guitar, and it appeared he had a natural talent for the instrument, which was amazing as no one else in either family had any musical inclinations or abilities. As he improved, Wayne finally bought him his own Gibson acoustic guitar in its own protective case. It became Eric's prized possession, and with his school practices and the endless hours he spent on the guitar at home, he became a very good and accomplished guitarist and musician. He really had an ear for music and could pick up tunes quite readily and play them back on his own guitar.

He recalled seeing Elvis Presley in his second movie **Loving You** a story of a nobody called Deke Rivers, an individual he could relate to, and who, in the movie, achieved fame and fortune as a new Singer and Entertainer. Well, in his own room, Eric became Deke Rivers as he belted out all the songs from the movie. Eric had grown into a lanky, hand-some, easy-going youth and stood over six foot tall. His hair was long, and just like Elvis, his hero, he too had sideburns.

His good looks and his gentle mannerism really impressed the girls, so he was never without a date for the school dances and the Friday night drive-ins.

Unexpectedly he started composing his own music and imitating much of the early fifties early rockabilly and southern blues music made so popular by the likes of the King, the Wild Southern Boy, Elvis Presley, Eddie Cochran, Ricky Nelson, Gene Vincent, Fats Domino, Jerry Lee Lewis, the Stray Cats, and Charlie Gracie and so many of the other fifties' entertainers. And to entertain himself, he started actually singing the actual songs and accompanying himself with his guitar, and accord-ing to his various girlfriends, they really loved his singing, and his guitar artistry.

At his local school, he actually performed at most of the school's sock hop dances, which the teenagers really enjoyed. With each dance, he got better and better and more confident with each appearance. Yes, as a handsome young teenager, he found that his guitar had brought many beautiful young girls to his side as he was always invited to parties organized by these young ladies. He himself was initially still a shy young teenager learning to live his life, but quite naive when it came to the "birds and the bees."

He needn't have worried as Jackie Shannon, a local bombshell Cheerleader and an astute organizer, and her Young Ladies Social Club quickly educated and taught him well in all the affairs of the heart and the sexual desires of the young ladies. Eric was a fast learner, and soon "the Nashville Rebel" was the guy all the hot young girls wanted to date for a night of passionate action. Eric was more than happy to facilitate the young ladies and their erotic dreams.

He loved the early Waylon Jennings's songs from the movie **Green River,** specially the song called "The Nashville Rebel." One night after the first time he sang the song at a school dance, the girls nicknamed him "The Nashville Rebel," and the name stuck!

> They call me the Nashville Rebel
> They said leave that Boy Alone
> Don't give him advice or he'll turn to ice
> And you might as well talk to stone

As Eric continued his song, he gyrated to the music on the stage, which the girls really liked.

> *But I've got things to do*
> *And things to say in my own way*

Eric just continued his song, surprised at the reaction he was getting specifically from the young ladies. He wasn't complaining.

> *I don't have time for your parties*
> *My love's little "guessing games"*
> *I've got songs to write in the still of*
> *the night*
> *I was born to write and sing*
> *And I've got things to do*
> *And things to say in my own way*

"Wow," the girls were all saying, "we got to have this guy! He's really cool on stage, and we love his singing, but what would he be like at a drive-in? We'll have to find out!"

> *They call me the Nashville Rebel*
> *Little girl don't you waste your time*
> *For I've given my heart to this old guitar*
> *You deserve a better love than mine...*
> *And I got...*

Yes, unknowingly Eric had become the desire of all the young ladies in school, the school's teen-age idol.

I'm the Nashville Rebel
I'm alone and I like it fine
I'd like to have a wife and live a normal life
But I just don't have the time
'Cause I've got...
        (Sung by Waylon Jennings)

Sexy and sultry brunette, Jackie Shannon, the head cheerleader at school, a vivacious brunette, virtually overnight, became his Social Manager as she arranged all his Friday Night Drive-ins and Saturday night parties, and she herself took great pleasure in teaching him all the ropes, so to speak, as she prided herself as an expert in passionate sex. And yes, she covered all the bases; nothing sexual was left out.

All his dates arranged by Jackie were with young ladies who were more than fully prepared to put out totally, orally, sexually, and yes, anally as well—and enthusiastically. Consequently, Eric was certainly not complaining, as they were all young and beautiful, so he got the cream of the crop. Eric too, was a quick learner, so with the vast variety of dates, his expertise in the pleasuring the young and mature ladies grew with each date and after each encounter.

Yes, as his reputation grew, and with Jackie's endorsements, quickly Eric received loads of invitations to numerous parties that the young ladies were organizing among themselves. Soon through the young girl's network, monitored through Jackie Shannon, he was invited to perform at the sock hops at the neighbouring schools districts as well, and soon "The Nashville Rebel" became well known as the local teen idol throughout his community and the Lexington region.

Eric was also good in sports as he was the wide receiver on his school's football team, and he also was on the school's basketball team and swim team. On the side, he also took martial arts training, and over a couple of years, he achieved his black belt status in both Tae Kwon Do and Karate. He had chosen to continue his lessons even after he had achieved both the black belts, basically to improve and refine what he had learnt and also to keep himself fit and in top physical condition.

Life appeared to be quite normal and quite relaxed. His Dad worked long hours, and his Mother, Jessie, had a part-time job, to keep herself occupied, at one of the local drugstores in Valley View.

Financially they were doing quite all right. They had a nice comfortable house with a swimming pool and two cars—a typical middle-class American family.

Then one night, Wayne, Eric's father, had taken Jessie and Eric into Richmond for a dinner treat, which was a pleasant change, as they typically always ate at home—fortunately Jessie was a good cook. They were a close-knit happy family and really had no problems.

On the way home to their small town of Valley View, driving along some almost deserted side roads outside of Richmond, unexpectedly a big Chrysler New Yorker pulled up behind them and slowly edged forward up to Wayne's Chevy and actually bumped his car several times. Wayne suddenly felt a chill down his back. This was not good!

"Wayne, slow down, Hun, and let him go by," suggested Jessie. So, Wayne slowed down, rolled down his window, and with his arm outside the car, he waved for the following car to pass him.

Then instantly the New Yorker pulled into the other lane and sped up, but as the car pulled level with their car, two revolvers appeared out of their windows as they blasted Wayne and Jessie in the front seat. Both were instantly dead, and their car swerved off the road into the lower ditch running parallel to the road. The car hit the soft dirt of the ditch, and with its forward motion, the wheels got caught in the soft dirt and instantly flipped the car over, which then rolled completely over again, several more times, but miraculously, on one flip, the back door swung open, and a body was flung out of the back seat of the car and landed clear away from where the car ultimately came to rest. Then when it finally came to rest upside down, there was a massive explosion as the car and contents where shredded into a million pieces.

There was nothing left of the car, the bodies of his parents, gone! How in world had Eric been flung out of the car, was a miracle in itself, and how in the hell had he survived this assault?

Obviously, Fate still needed Eric. His future was still ahead of him, and this Assault would not be forgotten. This was only the beginning of his trials and tribulations.

Chapter 3

The Accident

With the explosion and the following fire-ball, it didn't take long for the local police to show up on the scene, and when they found the unconscious bleeding body of a youth, they quickly established that he was still alive, and they immediately called in the ambulance that quickly transported him to the nearest hospital for immediate attention.

The Doctors were amazed he was still alive, especially from all the flying shrapnel and metal pieces and debris that blew out in all directions from the car during the explosion. They efficiently removed the applicable metal fragments embodied in him and quickly sewed up all his cuts to stop the bleeding, then placed his broken arm in a plaster cast. They took x-rays and several MRIs to determine what other injuries he had suffered, but fortunately as he had been in such excellent physical condition, he had no internal bleeding or damage to his vital organs. He did, however, have a broken arm. Yes, he was covered in bruises, numerous cuts that required stitches, but after a period of time, they too would fade away, and his scars would be hidden by clothing, except for those on his face. Those scars on his face were stitched carefully to minimize future visible scars showing.

The Doctors saw the scars on his back, and cringed, but said nothing, but that was from another time, and they had enough to do to patch up his existing wounds and to operate on his arm from this incident.

As Eric laid still and silently in the hospital bed, unexpectedly his Uncle Dwayne, his father's older arrogant brother walked into the hospital room. Looking at Eric, he laughed softly. He assumed Eric was asleep or still unconscious. Then almost emotionlessly and without thinking, he quietly spoke, thinking no one was close enough to hear what he was saying, but Eric, with his eyes closed, was actually awake, and he heard every word Dwayne had uttered in his snarling voice.

"You should have died in the crash too, kid. It would have made things a lot easier for all of us. Someone is now obliged to look after you, which was not in my plans at all, but as I am your only next of kin, that's a joke, regretfully for me, so legally that responsibility falls on me. Damn it."

"Let me tell you this is not my choice. They told me that all three of you would be taken care of, but somehow miraculously, the back door of your dad's car swung open, and you were flung out of the back seat, how, who knows how, but you were. Thus, the explosion didn't take care of business as it was supposed to. It left you still alive. Worst luck."

"So now you are my responsibility until you are eighteen, when I can officially kick you out into the big wide wonderful world. Until then, we'll just have to make the best of it as we can. Don't expect much. You won't get it. If it were up to me, you'd be out on the street on your own, right now. But the stupid authorities and useless laws said differently. But it appears that the hospital is planning to keep you for another week, which is fine with us. The longer, the better."

"Oh, sorry, too bad about your Dad, and unfortunately your Mom was just Collateral Damage, and you should have been too, but that's life! Even the best-laid plans don't always work out as one plans them. Right?" Dwayne laughed.

"Listen, your Dad, regretfully, was the problem. He just knew too much and had to be eliminated before he could talk to the Authorities, which he had threatened he would. He was not up to date with today's world and all the corruption, the deceit, and the eternal quest for money and more money. Stupidly he still believed in right and wrong, innocent and guilty, when we all know justice in America is really irrelevant and doesn't exist anymore. Hey, Man it's all about Money."

"Democracy, as per that stupid President of ours keeps telling everyone in the Middle East, is the key—key to what? We are selling Democracy there when we don't even have it here, in America. What a farce. Democracy left this country when he became President and regretfully that was long before." Dwayne laughed. "It's Money, Oil, and more Money, not for America. It's for themselves!

"Hey, buddy, we all...well, at least most of us know that in the United States, which in itself is a joke, we are not United. Anyway, we all know that Justice left for the Coast a long time ago and left America for some unknown destination. Also, the two-Party system in this country is a joke in itself. The two Parties can never agree on anything, so nothing ever happens. There is no Justice here anymore, only Money and more Money! Nothing else matters!

"You see, he, your Father, just didn't understand. He really was naive. Well, he won't have to worry about it now. Will he? He won't be talking to anyone now, will he?" Dwayne chuckled again.

"However, you—yes, you—are the lucky one, as you really know nothing, so you get to live a little longer. Not much longer, but a little longer."

"When the hospital finally releases you, you and your broken arm will stay at my place until I can figure out what to do with you. Damn it, why didn't you die like your Mom and Dad? It would have made things a lot easier. Now, damn it, I have to find a solution to my problem, and that problem is you, my dear nephew."

"Rest assured, I will find a way." He chuckled silently again.

Eric heard every word. Yes, he now knew that his arrogant Uncle was responsible for his loving Mother's and Father's deaths. Rest assured, there would be revenge—Eric would see to that. How? When? He didn't know, but he'd somehow find a way.

Revenge would be there. It was a promise and a commitment he made to himself. His Uncle Dwayne would pay for this one way or another. That is why Fate had made sure he remained alive.

Eric lay still, showing no emotions, no reaction, taking everything in that his Uncle had said. Yes, Uncle Dwayne was guilty of killing both his Mom and Dad, and he was also guilty of the attempted murder of Eric himself.

Then added to that, what Eric had not forgotten, was the murder of Dwayne's first wife, Olivia, back in Australia, which resulted in the brutal beating of Eric's back. No, Eric's brain made notes. Who Dwayne's accomplices were, Eric obviously didn't know, but he had their pictures in his brain. One way or another, he'd find them too, but his ultimate target was his Uncle Dwayne. He didn't know how long it would take him, but one way or another his Uncle and his insane wife, Alice would pay for this. Oh yeah, they would pay for this!

The question that haunted him was, what did his Father do to be killed like that? What did he know, that was so vital that he had to die, and his family too?

Perhaps, did the Package /letters in the safety deposit box that Wayne had given Eric, hold the keys and the clues as to why all this had happened?

Eric would find out soon enough!

Yes, there were many unanswered questions that needed to be resolved, and one way or another Eric's mind was already working overtime to determine what he could do to bring about closure to his Uncle and the Baldwin Organization.

Eric was convinced that the Package in the safety deposit box held, some of the answers to his many questions...yes, the Keys.

Chapter 4

The Family Support

On the day of his release from hospital, he was advised that since his arm was still in a plaster cast and since he still had many, many stitches in him, securing and healing all his multiple cuts that had been caused by all the shrapnel, the flying pieces of metal debris from the explosion, that he would certainly have to return to the hospital in three weeks' time to have, hopefully, the numerous stitches removed and to determine how his broken arm was healing. As the hospital was at capacity, they had to regretfully release him early, regretfully way too early!

Dwayne's obnoxious, buxom, vivacious, platinum-blonde ex-hooker and his second wife, Alice, who's attitude reflected that of her husband, picked Eric up from the hospital under protest. She wanted nothing to do with Eric.

Olivia, another vivacious and beautiful blonde, Dwayne's first wife, disappeared on a fishing expedition down in Australia. Apparently, she had fallen into a river infested with man-eating croc-odiles—her body was never recovered. Dwayne had blamed Eric, Wayne, his brother's son for pushing Olivia into the river and for also seducing his wife for passionate sex.

The real fact was that the beautiful Olivia did love the kind and considerate Eric, the only one she could trust, and yes , she had seduced the young handsome Eric and did have sex with Eric on numerous occasions, but Dwayne was none the wiser, and only guessed. He never had any proof that it did happen, so he made it up just to get rid of Olivia, who just wasn't as submissive as he would have liked her to be. Eric was the Scapegoat.

Dwayne took it out on Eric's back with his leather belt. Eric ended up in a hospital in Darwin for over three weeks recovering from the vicious leather belt assault on his back by Dwayne and Aldo, his right-hand man. Assault charges were pending, but Dwayne managed to slip out of the Australia, away from the Authorities, in a private Corporate jet.

Wayne and Jesse flew down to Australia to see Eric. Wayne never forgave Dwayne for his brutality and his lies and swore that one day he would get even. Eric did survive, but his back was scarred for life. Eric too swore revenge on Dwayne for killing the beautiful innocent Olivia and for the savage attack on him. Dwayne loved to hurt people and to see them suffer. He got his kicks in strange ways. Brutality was one of them.

In reality, Dwayne was a two-hundred-plus-pound fat slob and a complete coward, but as long as he controlled the money, he had others, like Aldo, to do his dirty work, and whenever Dwayne wanted to hurt someone, Aldo was there to hold them so they couldn't defend themselves, and more importantly, they could not strike back at Dwayne.

Dwayne was a sadistic egomaniac!

Alice was a class A platinum blonde hooker and a self-centred, spoilt bitch. It was obvious that she considered this situation a total inconvenience to her. Family connections or not, it was totally irrelevant to her. She never offered her condolences to Eric on the loss of his parents. All that was of no consequence. She never asked how he was or how he felt! There was no concern whatsoever. Nothing. Eric was no more than a pest that she was determined to get rid of. The fact that he looked more like Frankenstein again was irrelevant; there was no compassion no consideration for the injured youth.

The first thing she said was, "Look, kid, I didn't ask for this. I am not interested in charity! Baldwin family member or not, you are not my family so that is totally irrelevant! We are obligated to look after you for a while, so I am told by the authorities, but only until Dwayne sorts things out for you, so don't give me any shit or grief!"

"Understand?" she screamed.

"Yes, I understand, ma'am, and no, I won't give you any grief. Thank you for your help," added Eric, almost sarcastically.

So without saying another word, she drove him back to Eric's own house, where he had lived with his mom and dad. "Listen, kid, take what you want out of your house. You got five minutes."

The house had been totally ransacked, the furniture had all been turned upside down, the kitchen was in absolute shambles—everything was all over the place. It was as if someone were searching for something."

So quickly Eric grabbed his small bag, threw some clothes and shoes into it, his small portable radio, and then he grabbed his trusty guitar in its case, checked its condition, which hadn't been touched, fortunately, and headed out back to her Cadillac.

That night their house burnt down—arson, so it was determined! It was obvious that whatever they were looking for, they hadn't found or alternatively had never existed. The insurance company covered the loss of the house, and within the week, the property was sold. Everything was handled by Dwayne, Eric had no input into anything, although technically Eric was the beneficiary of the Estate of Wayne and Jesse Baldwin, but no one was going to argue with Dwayne.

There was no funeral or church service, for his parents as the explosion and the subsequent fire had destroyed everything. There were no bodies to bury or burn. It was as simple as that.

So with his guitar and his small bag, Alice the Bitch drove him back to their mansion and set him up in one of the small maid's quarters.

At Dwayne's mansion, Alice showed Eric to his quarters. "This is where you will live for as long as you are here, I'll get the staff to bring you a small TV. Don't wander around the house. Use the staff's washroom. Look, I don't want to see you at all. So stay in this room as much as possible. Remember, this is not your house, it's mine. You are only a temporary unwanted guest."

"Yes, ma'am, I'll be as invisible as possible."

"Also, I guess you'll be heading back to school tomorrow, eh?" she inquired with her perpetual sneer on her face.

"Yes, ma'am, I guess so!" responded Eric.

"So basically, you'll be only sleeping here at night, right?"

"Yes, ma'am."

Next morning at school, Eric fronted up at the Office of the Principal, who was absolutely shocked to see him at school, specifically in the condition he was still in, but obviously, Alice, his Aunt, could have cared less, as she just dropped him off.

The Principal offered his condolences on the deaths of his Mother and Father.

"Are you all right, son? I would have thought that your Aunt and Uncle would have kept you home for another two to three weeks at least, but

I guess some people just don't have any feelings for others, regretfully. Listen, if it is too much for you, you can go and lie down in the nurse's room for as long as you like, okay? I'll talk to the nurse. She'll take care of you."

"Thank you, sir, I appreciate it. I think it would be better. Otherwise, I might be frightening some of the young ladies in my Frankenstein costume, I think," responded Eric with a smile.

So for the next two weeks, the school nurse, Miss Holstein, looked after Eric and kept him out of sight as much as possible. The school provided him lunch and drinks at no cost to him.

At school, initially all the kids came over when they first saw him and were very sympathetic and offered their condolences to him. They were absolutely shocked and actually horrified at what they saw. His handsome face was a mess. He really did look more like Frankenstein, with his cuts, stitches, and bruises all over his face and body, and his one arm still in a cast. But they were very respectful and never asked any questions, which Eric appreciated. They basically left him alone.

The girls he had dated were actually scared to go near him, as their bodies reacted to the horror that they saw when they looked at him. In reality, if he wasn't living with his Aunt and Uncle, his own Parents would have kept him home until his cuts had healed, the stitches had been removed, and the bruises had started to disappear, but his sadistic, indifferent Aunt and Uncle just didn't give a damn and basically were pissed off that he hadn't died in the crash.

*   *   *

A couple of weeks later, when Dwayne arrived back home, he met with Eric, who had just been fed in his own room by one of the Mexican maids.

"Listen, Eric," said Dwayne casually, "we have sold the house, the property. The insurance provided us a compensation package, your Dad's life insurance policy was paid out, and there is a severance package that Grandad set up, so there were some additional funds there. So I opened up an account with the Chase Manhattan Bank in town for you, and we have deposited all the applicable funds due to you into it.

"Here's your account book, but you'll have to go to town tomorrow to fill in the applicable forms. Okay?" Dwayne laughed.

"Yes, okay, thank you, Uncle."

Eric checked the account balance, which showed exactly $100, which was what Eric expected. So Dwayne had killed his Parents and now had stripped him, his own Nephew, financially clean as well. As if he needed the money. The Bastard! Eric said nothing. He knew it would serve no purpose, and he'd probably be clobbered if he did.

What Dwayne didn't know was that Wayne's funds had already been transferred into Eric's account at their own bank, a bank that Dwayne knew nothing about. So Eric's account was actually, now with the transfer, well over $500,000.00

"As you have noticed, I had to deduct my commission for doing all these things for you, and of course room and board here," said Dwayne as he walked away laughing out loud. Suddenly he turned around and came back.

"How old are you now, Eric?"

"I am seventeen, and I'll be eighteen in a couple of months, sir."

"Excellent, so as soon as you turn eighteen, you and your guitar are out of here, Understand?"

"Yes, sir," responded Eric.

"And don't bother to ask me any questions about your Dad. You won't get any answers. Understand?"

"Perfectly."

The first weekend, Eric disappeared into town and avoided Alice and Dwayne basically all weekend. Friday and Saturday nights, he slept in the local park with the Homeless. It was obvious that his Aunt and Uncle hated him. Why? He didn't know, but frankly the reasons were irrelevant. The two brothers had worked together with Eric's grandfather, Alberto, until he passed away.

After that, there was never any family get-togethers. Dwayne and Alice had nothing to do with Jessie and Wayne—or Eric, for that matter. Why? Eric never knew.

But now with his Mom and Dad dead, it was all irrelevant anyway. And Eric now knew that Dwayne was responsible for their deaths, and at some time Eric would come back to even the score. But Eric also realized that Dwayne was intent on getting rid of him as well. When or how, he obviously had no idea.

Then inexplicably one afternoon, having just returned from school, suddenly Alice stormed into his room, screaming her head off. "I am so sick of having you in this house, you son of a bitch! I want you out of here now! When Dwayne gets in, he'll take care of you, you little shit!"

Eric was shocked. He had had no communications with Alice whatsoever since he arrived, as he had stayed in his room all night, watching TV, or playing his guitar. What the hell was her problem? Eric had no clue. The sadistic bitch had to be off her rocker, without a doubt, insane!

One of the cute Caribbean maids had said to him, privately and quietly, when she had brought his dinner into his small room, "Hey, Baby, it's not just you, Eric. She treats all of us like that."

The Caribbean native servants were treated like slaves and continually verbally abused by both Alice and Dwayne, but obviously more specifically by Alice. Dwayne was intelligent enough to understand and ordered Alice accordingly that, never, under any circumstance, could she hit any of the servants physically.

"Yell and scream at them as much as you want, but never, never, ever touch them, Alice. Please understand. If you do, you are out of here. I just don't need the FBI in here, understand?"

"Yes, Baby, of course," purred Alice with her fake plastered-on smile.

She followed Dwayne's Orders, but she was so often tempted to strike out at the female servants. All of them absolutely hated her, and she knew it. They had reason to. Alice was an outright sadistic bitch.

Chapter 5

Abandoned

Suddenly an hour later, Dwayne barged into the room. "Grab your guitar, Kid. We are out of here!"

So quickly Eric put his guitar back in its case and closed it, then grabbed his few clothes and threw them in his small bag and headed out the door to the waiting Cadillac. Eric climbed into the back seat with his bag and guitar and found Dwayne sitting beside him. Another unknown man to Eric was the Driver. Minutes later, they drove out of the circular driveway out onto the street and immediate headed out of the city limits out into the deserted country roads.

Eric never said a word, never asked any questions. He just sat there quietly. Whatever would be, would be. It was now totally beyond his control. Would they finally eliminate him as well? He, of course, had no idea that Fate would determine his life now. Perhaps he would be joining his Mom and Dad tonight!

So on a deserted side road, the Cadillac came to a halt. Instantly Dwayne jumped out of the car, along with the Driver.

"Get out, kid," said Dwayne aggressively. "We've finally come to the end of the road."

Then as Eric climbed out of the car, Dwayne grabbed his guitar case and flung it into the depressed ditch along side the road. His small bag followed, and Dwayne and the Driver laughed. Yes, they really appeared to be enjoying themselves. Weird! What had Eric ever done to them or that bitch, Alice?

Nothing! Absolutely nothing!

Then almost expecting it, the Driver grabbed Eric and held his arms behind his back, as Dwayne suddenly began to punch Eric viciously and obviously with the intent to kill him. With his arms being held back, he couldn't even defend himself as Dwayne continued the savagely assaulting him, blow after blow. The Driver even held his broken arm back so the Dwayne wouldn't hit his cast on his arm. The stiches from his wounds from the car accident, all came loose as blood began to sleep from his previous wounds. His nose started to bleed as well, but fortunately it was not broken. His face again was badly bruised. Then Dwayne switched to punching his body and using it like a boxer's training bag. Finally, the Driver released Eric, and he collapsed and fell to the side of the road.

All through the assault, Eric never screamed, never uttered a word, but took all the blows that they had they had handed out. How he was still alive and still conscious was really amazing, but his willpower kept him going.

On the side of the road, the two men continued to kick him savagely as if it was just a great game for them, as they continued to laugh. Yes, the intent was to kill him, an innocent kid who had nothing to do with them at all. His face was now all covered with blood, and he was barely breathing. Finally, Dwayne stuck his foot under Dwayne and flicked him into the ditch beside his faithfully guitar and case.

Down in the muddy ditch, Eric, lying in the mud, still conscious, looked up at the two laughing men through his swollen face, his eyes just about closed from the swellings. But his brain saw enough and photographed two images that would always be there.

"I think we have seen the last of him, Boss," said Aldo with a smile.

"Yes, I hope so, Aldo. Damn, I wish he had died in that crash, but this time I doubt he will last long now. Let's get out of here!"

So they climbed back into the Caddie and drove off, leaving Eric supposedly to die in the ditch.

After they had left, Eric tried to stand up. He hurt all over. He tried several times until he managed to stay up. He was still bleeding all over. His face was a mess, covered with blood and swollen badly. In reality, it was amazing he was still alive.

Slowly he began to crawl up from the ditch, dragging his guitar case with him. It was the only thing that mattered to him now. If he was going to die, it would be holding his guitar. How he had managed to crawl up the embankment to the surface of the road was incredible and frankly in his fragile condition, inconceivable. But he did!

The fact was, prior to the car accident, he had been in great physical shape, but with the car accident, he had lost some of his strength and stamina, and now with this vicious assault and beating handed out by Dwayne, his own Uncle, and his driver, Aldo his body was completely sapped. His stamina and fortitude were gone. He was totally beaten to the edge of termination. The only thing he had left was his self-determination to survive. He had to survive to be able to repay the debt that he now owed to his Uncle and his Accomplishers.

He knew what he had to do. His body was beaten, but his brain continued his struggle to stay alive.

He had to stay alive so he could revenge his Mother and Father, and indirectly Olivia.

He had to!

Fate had decided. This was not over yet!

Chapter 6

The Wind Crest Hills Estate

Eric staggered ever so slowly on that deserted roadway, one step at a time, in the darkness, going where, he had no clue. He certainly didn't know. He was miles from any civilization. His body was convinced it would soon be over. Only his brain still functioned, determined to keep him alive.

Finally, Fate stepped in. This had gone far enough!

Fate had taken control. Eric would survive, and sometime in the future he would put things right.

Quite unexpectedly, the tide began to change. Mr. and Mrs. Alycia and Allen Taylor, the Owners of the expansive Wind Crest Hills Thoroughbred Estate, were taking a shortcut home from a party that they had just attended with some close friends.

It was dark, and the road was deserted, but suddenly up ahead in the headlights, Alycia saw somebody staggering along the road, and it looked like he was dragging a guitar case behind him.

Then suddenly as they came closer, the figure collapsed again onto the road.

"Stop, Allen, maybe we should stop and call 911. Whoever it is certainly looks like he needs both the police and the ambulance."

As soon as Allen had stopped, Alycia jumped out of the car and ran up to the figure on the road and turned him over onto his back. As soon as she saw his face, she screamed loudly, shocked at the horror and terror before her.

"Oh my god, it's a young man, and it looks like he's been beaten to a pulp. Who would do such a horrible thing? God, Allen, I'm amazed he is still alive. Let's call 911. Allen, he needs help. Badly!"

Then quite unexpectedly, they heard a soft voice pleading.

"No, ma'am, please don't do that. I'll be okay. No police. No ambulance. I was there two weeks ago. I know who beat me up, and if he finds out that I am still alive, he will try to kill me again," said Eric with a raspy voice, his mouth and face still bleeding. Both his eyes were almost closed from the swellings. His lips were cracked, bleeding, his face covered in blood.

Alycia shivered, imagining what the rest of his body would look like.

"Well, Son. We are not leaving you here. If we do, you will surely die," said Alycia, all concerned for this youth. She could not believe what they had done to him.

"Perhaps, ma'am, perhaps that would be the best," responded Eric with difficulty.

"No way, Kid, we are taking you home with us," said Allen. So quickly Alycia and Allen lifted him into the back of their van and placed his guitar case beside him. His few clothes remained in the mud in the ditch. Then they sped home.

As soon as they reached their Estate, Allen jumped out of the car and immediately called their family Doctor, James Adams, who they had known for year. They asked him to come over to their place as quick as possible, as there was a serious problem that they needed him for, and to bring his special bag. This was not a social visit.

"Sure, Allen, I'll be right over," confirmed the Doctor

Then Allen called Greg, his ranch manager, and Bill, in charge of the stables, another of the Estate hands to help them lift the Kid into one of their spare guest rooms. They too could not believe the beating that this young man had received, and they too wondered what was keeping him alive. Alycia had already covered one of the beds with an old vinyl shower curtain and numerous old towels, and they laid him down there. Together they managed to get all his mud-covered clothes off him and to take his shoes off as well.

When they removed his shirt, they discovered his back was scarred severely, obviously from a previous beating. "Oh My God, this poor Kid has been to hell and back several times. Just look at his back, Allen. This is just unbelievable. How can people be so cruel?" said Alycia, almost in tears.

Slowly Eric opened his eyes, looked around the room at all the concerned faces, and smiled.

"Thank you, folks, thank you," he said softly, relieved. The horror and pain from the assault was behind him.

Then suddenly, Kiara, the beautiful blonde daughter of the Taylors, walked into the room.

Eric smiled. "Oh yeah, I think I just entered heaven. You know, I just saw this beautiful blonde Angel, yes, a gorgeous blonde Angel that obviously could only live in Heaven," said Eric softly, almost whispering as a smile returned to his face. Then slowly he lost consciousness and blacked out.

"Oh, my God, Mom. Did he just die?" inquired their beautiful fifteen-year-old daughter, Kiara.

"No, Darling, he just blacked out. No, he's still alive. It's just that he has just been to hell for the second time, but he is back now, and he is just asleep for a while," said Alycia.

"Oh, Thank God! Hey, I looked at his guitar case, and there was a name on it. He is Eric Baldwin."

"That's great, Hun. Now we will be able to tell Dr. Adams just who he is. Eric Baldwin." Then she thought for a minute. "Hey, Allen! Wait a minute... Baldwin, Baldwin...Could this be the same boy whose parents were blown up in that car accident two weeks ago, and their son was miraculously thrown out of the car before it blew up?"

"Alycia, I think you are right. The Baldwin family has long been associated with the Mob for years, so perhaps the Family was also trying to eliminate Eric as well. That would also explain the cast on his arm and the stitches on his face, arms, and legs and other parts of his body. God, it really is a wonder he has survived this far. But the question is, who beat him up? I'm guessing it had to be his Uncle, or men that are working for his Uncle. He said he knew who had done this, didn't he?"

"Yes, Hun, he did," confirmed Alycia.

As Allen and Greg vacated the room to discard all his mud- and blood-covered clothes, carefully Alycia, with Kiara's help, washed the mud off his now naked body, and the pair of them could not miss the fact that the youth was certainly well endowed. Alycia looked at him and then at Kiara, and they both smiled.

Wow, they both thought, wow, this youth is certainly well equipped.

Alicia and Kiara took turns gently handling him and washing him clean. They were thrilled that his body was actually responding to their gentle caresses and strokes. Yes, Alycia and Kiara were impressed.

While they all waited for the Dr. Adams, Alycia had a bowl of warm water as she washed the remaining blood from Eric's face and arms. She noticed that his left arm was broken and still in a cast, but the cast was bent! Many of the stitches on the cuts had been broken, and the cuts had opened up again and were weeping with more blood. His whole body was bruised purple from all the kicks delivered by Aldo and Dwayne. Alycia had covered the remainder of his body with some clean old towels to keep him somewhat warm.

"Jesus, Alycia, I'm calling our friend Jake Sanders, who is an FBI Agent. This is getting to be very complicated, but first we have to do whatever we can for this young man here," said Allen.

"Yes, we do, Dad," said Kiara softly. "God, they have really beaten him up, haven't they, Dad? Why?" questioned Kiara as she looked at poor Eric sadly. "Who would do such a horrible thing?"

Despite her young age, Kiara was really anxious to help in any way she could. Inexplicably Kiara realized that Fate had told her that this young man was to play an important role in her life. Who he was, was irrelevant. She surprisingly really felt for him. There was something special about him that she could not explain. She instinctively knew that they would be close.

"Oh, Dr. Adam's on his way and should be here any minute," advised Allen. "And I am going to call Jake right now as well. He really needs to see this. "

Chapter 7

His Father's Secret

Some weeks earlier, his Father, Wayne, had taken Eric aside and advised him that he had set up a separate Account at the local branch of the Bank of America and had deposited $25,000 into the account, just in case something were to happen to him.

"Also, my joint account with Jesse at the same bank has almost $500,000, or thereabouts in it, and you are the beneficiary of that Account, as well, if anything were to happen to Me or Mom," said Wayne, almost as a prediction of something that was to happen.

It made Eric very uneasy as well, but he never said a word.

In addition, he handed Eric a thick package with a stack of documents in it, about an inch thick, which he asked Eric to deposit in one of the Bank's safety deposit boxes, which he told Eric not to open.

"If something was to happen to me, then take this letter to the FBI, not the local police, but the FBI, okay?"

"Sure, Dad, but why? What is in this envelope? What is going on?" inquired Eric.

"Look, Eric, you are grown up now, and you know sometimes things happen that you seemingly have no control over, strange things that one cannot avoid. Well, things have happened, and I have no control over them. Also, if they discover I have heard certain things, then I am in trouble as well. I don't know what the consequences would be, and at this point, they don't know that I know. That is all I can say at this time. But don't you open the package now. Let the FBI deal with it at the appropriate time. The real fact is, the less you know right now, the better it is for you and Mom. So let's put the letter in a safety deposit box, and we'll have you sign your Account Documents to set up the Account."

"These people you keep calling 'they.' Who are they?"

"Eric, you know who they are, and who is in charge."

"Yes, of course, I know." He didn't need to be told. He already knew. It was his arrogant crooked Uncle Dwayne, Eric knew only too well that his Uncle could not be trusted. His Dad worked for the Organization ever since his Grandad was around, but when he passed away, Dwayne took over the operations, and everything changed, but Wayne kept his mouth shut. Eric knew Dwayne was dangerous, and whatever he was doing was against the law. Why else was his Dad doing this? Suddenly a cold chill ran down Eric's back as he feared for the life of his Father.

"Be careful, Dad, and watch your back."

"Well, Time and Fate would tell."

Now time certainly had told him. Both his Dad and his Mom were both dead, and it appeared that Dwayne wanted him dead as well. What was in the package in the safety deposit box. Eric had no idea, no clue, but he was sure that it had to do with Dwayne's operations and the Baldwin's Corporation's future plans.

Now there was only him left—Eric Baldwin. Eric had kept his word. He hadn't said a word to anyone, not even his own Mom, God bless her!

But strangely, a cold wind blew over his head, and he knew deep down that something was going to happen to his Dad, but regretfully he was in no position to help his Father or avoid the inevitable conclusions.

Chapter 8

The Doctor's Visit

As soon as Dr. James Adams arrived, Allen quickly ushered him into the spare room where Eric lay unconscious on the bed. Kiara sat beside him, surprisingly holding his hand, and Eric was holding hers.

"Oh, my God, oh my God, is he still alive?"

"His name is Eric Baldwin. It was on his guitar case," advised Alycia.

"Okay, let me have a look at him and let me clean up all his wounds." But looking at the condition Eric was in, Dr. Adams changed his mind. "On second thought, I think the best thing would be for me to take him to my Private Clinic, where we can clean him up properly and much faster. Then we can take x-rays and several MRI's of his head, as he has really taken such a savage beating."

"James, before I called you, he asked us not to call the police or the ambulance and that he knew who beat him up, and he said that if his Uncle found out that he was still alive, they would probably try to kill him again," said Allen.

"Oh, I see, well if this is the same boy who escaped the car bomb two weeks ago—and from the previous scars and broken stitches, I would suggest he is—then it is a miracle he is still alive. God, his Uncle and Aunt obviously have no hearts at all, and to do this to this young man, this is just unbelievable. Yeah, let's get him to My Clinic. I'll get several other doctors to help me, then we can assess what else needs to be done. I think that plaster case on his arm may need to be replaced after I see the x-rays. We may have to re-operate on his arm again, if the settings have changed, which appears to be the case. Irrespective, the cast is bent and needs to be replaced anyway. Then I can also check with the other doctors who treated him two weeks ago, confidentially, of course. I would suggest we have him change his name so no one will know who he is.

"God, Alycia and Allen, thank God you found him when you did. I haven't seen such a savage beating in years. I'm amazed that he is still alive. God, did you see his back? Obviously from another time. How he survived such brutality is just amazing."

After several injections, Dr. Adams called his own Clinic to prepare them for Eric's arrival. Quickly from his car, James brought in a special emergency-type blanket and, with Allen's and Alycia's help James, wrapped up Eric in it and quickly carried him to Allen's Suburban. Immediately James attached an oxygen mask on Eric as a precaution. As Dr. Adams was quickly leading the way, Allen followed him to his private Clinic. In the back of the Suburban, Alycia and Kiara sat there to make sure that Eric remained calm and that his condition remained the same. He was still unconscious.

Alycia was amazed that Kiara was taking such an interest in this young man's condition. It was as if Kiara already knew him. It was weird, but Alycia said nothing, as she too acknowledged that there was something special about this young man, that she too also felt an attraction toward him. Fate had created two beautiful Allies for Eric.

In the Clinic, Dr. James Adams and his team went to work, cleaning his body thoroughly, removing all the broken stiches, redressing all his previous and new wounds. The x-ray proved that the arm had to be reset, and a new cast would be required. Dr. Adams performed the operation and the resetting of his arm bones accordingly, himself. A new cast was applied to his arm. His condition fortunately remained stable, but after all his wounds and bruises were taken care of, it was mandatory that he remain at the clinic's care for at least the next two to three weeks, if not longer, obviously depending on the speed of his recovery. Dr. Adams would monitor his condition daily, and he would reassess Eric's condition after the two to three weeks of proper care.

While Allen, Alycia, and Kiara sat patiently in the waiting area, Jake Sanders, the FBI agent and close friend of Allen, also showed up at the clinic after Allen had called him. Allen then relayed all that had happened since they found poor Eric on the deserted side road, to Jake, who could not believe it, but he was not surprised.

"Yeah, for some reason, Wayne Baldwin was killed by his own brother—why, we don't know. Eric and his Mother, Jessie, were expected to be just Collateral Damage. Obviously, there was no care for the Family." Jake then advised Allen, Alycia, and Kiara about the so-called arson on their house. "And I understand that Dwayne has sold the property, etc., as well. I also understand that Eric's inheritance of Wayne's and Jessie's estate is exactly $100. That is all. Also, I would be safe in saying that Dwayne himself was the one who beat up Eric, probably along with some help.

"I don't know for sure, but it appears as if they, Dwayne and the Taurus Corporation, were looking for something. The house, according to one of our Agents, had been totally ransacked, which would suggest they were, in fact, searching for something. Perhaps Eric has some information that might explain these things. Perhaps Wayne, his father, took him into his confidence and told him something.

"Whenever Eric is well enough, I'd like to talk to him. Also, I agree with Dr. Adams that Eric should definitely change his name as soon as possible, and his visit here to this Clinic be under a different name. If Eric knows who beat him up, then we have to make sure that Eric Baldwin is never heard from again. If one of you talks to him first, suggest the new name issue with him. And Alycia, Kiara, and you, Allen, need to be thanked for helping Eric at his time of need. As Dr. Adams will tell you, if you all hadn't helped him when you did, he would have now been with his Mom and Dad, for sure."

It was almost two hours later that Dr. Adams finally resurfaced.

"Well, folks, we have him back in a stable condition and breathing normally. Let me tell you, though, your prompt action saved this young man's life last night. If you hadn't found him when you did, he'd now be dead, without question, which I really believe was his Uncle's intent."

"Yeah, I think it best when he wakes up, he selects a new name for himself so we can record what we have done here today under a different name. Eric Baldwin will just disappear!"

Chapter 9

The FBI Secret Agent

Something that Jake Sanders did tell the Taylors was that when the FBI had heard about the mysterious car crash and explosion and deaths of Wayne and Jessie Baldwin and that their son Eric had miraculously survived, immediately the FBI had his hospital room bugged, and when Dwayne, his Uncle, came to visit Eric, he carelessly had self-confessed to the murder of Wayne and Jessie Baldwin and the attempted murder of Eric Baldwin. It was all recorded on tape. Now the FBI had positive proof of the murder, but they now held off until they could establish why Wayne had been scheduled for elimination.

What did Wayne know that prompted Dwayne Baldwin to become so scared, and what made it so important and imperative to eliminate him before he could talk?

Obviously, Dwayne and Wayne had had some form of conversation about what was going on within their corporation, and obviously the two brothers had not agreed on some or certain issues. What were those issues?

Several weeks earlier...

"Look, Dwayne, don't be stupid. If you proceed with these plans, you'll put everyone of us under suspicion, including all the members of our families. Look, we are not 'Murder Incorporated.' Our business is not killing people!"

"Look, Wayne, I really don't give a damn about you or your family, never have. Understand? I run this organization, and everyone takes orders from me. Yes, you are the Consigliere, the one that provides advice, but I am the Don, and I don't have to listen to anything you might want to say. So what I think as far as you are concerned is totally irrelevant. Do I make myself clear? So take my advice stay out of it. None of this concerns you.

"Understand, Wayne, I know you are well aware of what our plans are, both short term and long term, but if you have any objections, keep them to yourself, understand? If you don't, then I will not be responsible if something were to happen to Jessie, Eric, and, yes, you, for that matter," roared Dwayne.

"So now you are threatening me and my family? Dwayne, you might be the Don, but might I remind you, I am Family too, and so are Jessie and Eric. I don't think New York would be pleased with your interpretation of Family Code," responded Wayne defiantly.

"New York is not involved. We run our own shows down here in the South. New York has no control over what we do. Remember, their Family is not our Family. So, Wayne, Brother or not, keep your mouth shut and stay clear of our operations, and finally I make all the decisions. You, Wayne, are our Accountant, so stick to the crunching the numbers racket and stay out of our business operations, or there will be consequences," concluded Dwayne angrily.

Dwayne now realized he had a problem. It was obvious that Wayne had feelings for others, whereas Dwayne didn't care for anyone except himself. Even Alice could be easily replaced and could disappear at the drop of the hat, if necessary. She serviced him, at this point satisfactorily, that was all. There was no love involved between the two of them.

The simple truth was that Wayne knew too much, and if he were to talk, say, to the FBI, then there could be serious consequences and would totally disrupt the Baldwin operations.

But not surprisingly, with the turmoil in the Federal Government, there were certainly Politicians starting to look at and planning to take out, some of the Political Figures that were threatening the Super Rich's gravy trains of the United States. This was taking the Baldwin organization totally in a different direction, and the connections and repercussions would be very far reaching right across the country.

And the fact was, Wayne was well aware of that, and that was what scared Dwayne.

This was not the mandate of any Mafia operation, this was not their speciality, this was just another bright idea from Dwayne. Dwayne also now realized that the Politicians supporting the Super Rich would be prepared to pay big bucks to eliminate some of the undesirables—yes, big bucks!

*   *   *

Eric was going nowhere until Dr. Adams himself agreed to have him released from his care. He was scheduled to remain in the private clinic for at least two to three weeks, longer if it was deemed necessary by Dr. Adams and his staff.

As soon as Jake Sanders was advised by Dr. Adams that Eric was awake and could talk, he came to visit him. The next day he was there. Jake was shown to his room.

When Jake walked into Eric's room at Dr. Adams's clinic, he introduced himself.

"Good afternoon, Eric," said Jake. "I am Jake Sanders, a good friend of Allen and Alycia Taylor, but more importantly, I am also an FBI Special Agent. They had called me just after they found you. When I was talking to them, they mentioned that you had told them that you knew who had beaten you up."

"Please to meet you, Sir. I am glad that you have come, as I too needed to talk to you and the FBI. This is good. By the way, at everyone's suggestions and recommendations, I have changed my name to an indiscreet name, Chris Canyon. Eric Baldwin no longer exists."

"That's great news, Chris, we don't want to let anyone know what happened to Eric Baldwin, specifically not your Uncle. This will make the issues easier. Don't worry, the FBI will arrange that all the legal documents concerning your identity are all revised for you, and those papers that need your signature I will bring to you, personally."

"Okay, just for your information, when you were in hospital before, your Uncle Dwayne Baldwin entered your room and virtually self-confessed killing your parents and trying to kill you. Well, we have that conversation on tape."

"Yes, good, I was awake when he said that. He obviously thought I was unconscious or asleep. I wasn't, but he didn't know."

"But there was something else nobody knew about," suggested Chris. "There was a thick package/envelope Dad gave me. It is in my safety deposit box at the Bank, and it is addressed for the FBI."

"A letter for the FBI? What kind of envelope was that, Chris?" inquired Jake, suddenly excited.

"An envelope/package, and I assume a stack of Documents my Dad had left for the FBI, and it is about an inch thick!"

"Really?" responded Jake. Perhaps this was what Dwayne was looking for, perhaps these Documents were what Dwayne was searching for, and perhaps they would explain exactly why Wayne and his wife, Jesse, were murdered and why Eric was also expected to die.

Now everything rested with the letter that Wayne had given to Eric and who, without opening the letter, had placed it in the safety deposit box at the Bank of America, where he and Wayne, his Dad, had opened an account in his name.

With the confirmed deaths of Wayne and Jessie, his parents, the funds in their joint account were now transferred automatically over to Eric's account, and after Jake's visit to the bank, the name Eric Baldwin, disappeared and was replaced by Chris Canyon.

*   *   *

"Look, Jake, several weeks before Mom and Dad were assassinated, Dad took me aside one day. I noticed he was very nervous. Then he confided in me, and basically, I became very aware he was scared for his life. We opened up a new account for me at the Bank of America branch in Valley View, but more importantly he gave me a thick manila envelope full of numerous documents. The envelope was sealed and Labelled 'FBI.' He told me that should something happen to him, that I was to turn that envelope over to you folks, but definitely *not* to the local Police Force. He told me not to open the envelope, as the less I knew, the safer I would be.

"So I placed the envelope addressed to the FBI in my safety deposit box, unopened. But as My Dad was the Taurus Corporation's Accountant, he obviously knew many things that my Uncle would have preferred him not knowing. Anyway, I never opened it, so I really have no idea what is in there, but Dwayne, my Uncle was aware that something was missing, I suspect. And yes, it was My Uncle Dwayne who beat-me up with the intent that I would die in the deserted roadside ditch.''

"Like I said, I never opened the package or read what was in there, so I have no idea what to expect. The safety deposit key is attached to the head of my guitar, which is my only procession now, and is on my bunk at the Wind Crest Hills Estate. I am so grateful for all that Mr. and Mrs. Taylor and their gorgeous young daughter, Kiara, have done for me. It's like they have been my guardian angels.''

"So listen, Jake, I suggest you go to their Estate and get them to give you the key off my guitar and have them turn it over to you. Then get the package/letter from the Bank safety deposit box. After you find out what is in the envelope, I would appreciate also knowing why my father was such a threat to my Uncle and his organization and why he was eliminated,'' concluded Chris. "I really expect that the documents will explain many issues.''

"I am sure these documents will be very interesting, and you are right, I expect they will explain why your Parents were killed and why your Uncle wanted you out of the way as well.''

"I have a debt to pay before I am done, Jake. I have decided to join the Navy Seals program when I am eighteen and become a Navy SEAL Operative for a period of time. Then when I return, I will be a new man, and I will be ready to disrupt Dwayne's operations," confided Chris.

"Chris, just remember, I too still have numerous debts to pay back to your Uncle Dwayne Baldwin, the Taurus Organization, as well, so perhaps you and I can tackle and resolve those debts together. As I am with the FBI, I will be able to provide you with all the backup you will need to deal with your Uncle."

"Sounds like a plan, Jake. It's a deal."

Then together they called Allen, and Chris confirmed that it was okay for Allen to take the safety deposit box key off his guitar and to give it to Jake.

"Chris, I'll make sure that Jake gets it. Thank God I brought him into this scenario," responded Allen as he personally went and got the key, then he waited for Jake to show up.

Jake said farewell to Chris, and he immediately headed for the Wind Crest Hills Thoroughbred Estate to get the safety deposit box key.

"By the way, Chris, Alycia and Kiara are apparently on their way to see you as well, and they should be here within ten minutes or so, according to Allen."

"Thanks, Mr. Sanders, thanks for everything."

"Hey, kid, it's okay. Remember and appreciate that we, you and I, still have lots to do, and after we see your Dad's documents, there will be a lot more to do, I am sure of it, but what we will find out. I'm sure it will be very interesting. Your Uncle will keep for the time being, but rest assured we will bring him down."

* * *

Shortly after Jake left, Kiara and Alycia came into his room. Kiara rushed over to Chris and immediately hugged him gently, then softly kissed his bruised lips, and Alycia kissed the side of his face that wasn't bandaged up. Then Kiara took his hand and held it firmly, which was something she did now regularly whenever she came to visit him.

"Don't you worry about anything. We will look after you, especially me," said Kiara with a great big smile on her face, which warmed Chris's heart. He was really impressed by Kiara. She treated him as if she was his girlfriend. In her own mind, she really already was.

Chapter 10

The Informative Package

After retrieving the key to Chris's safety deposit box, Jake immediately drove to the Bank of America branch in Valley View and retrieved the thick envelope addressed to the FBI by Wayne Baldwin, Chris's father. Jake took the envelope back to headquarters and, carefully, with the Director of the FBI Branch, several agents familiar with the Baldwin's organization, and several FBI lawyers, spent several days going over the documents and slowly formulating a plan of attack.

The Director had called in the State Governor and the State's legal beavers as well, and together they planned their course of action relative to the corruption in the local Lexington City Hall and the Lexington Police Force. Two platoons of national guards were called in to maintain law and order.

Then on that specific day, there were simultaneous applicable Raids on the Lexington City Hall and the Lexington Police Department and all the applicable individuals whose names appeared on the documents turned over by Wayne to the FBI were automatically and systematically arrested.

After the State Authorities and the FBI had carried out their Raids and all the applicable individuals were arrested or placed on house arrest, at that point Jake Sanders came in to see Chris. For the next several hours, Chris listened intently as Jake explained all that had happened.

Several days later, when Alycia, Allen, and Kiara were visiting Dr. Adam's clinic, Chris brought the Taylors up to date with contents of the envelope that his Dad had left for the FBI

"Just for your information, before Dad was killed, he left me a thick package/envelope, which was about an inch thick, with numerous documents in it, and said that I should give to the FBI, and not the local Police, if anything happened to him. Well, when Jake Sanders came in, I told him about the envelope and where he could find it. I understand he got the safety deposit box key from my guitar from you and has already retrieved the letter from the bank.

"Well, apparently, the envelope contained numerous very damaging, incriminating letters about our corrupt Politicians at City Hall and Police Department Officials, our Judges and Prosecutors, even our Mayor. So the FBI planned simultaneous raids on the Lexington Town Hall and the Lexington Police Departments. Also, the FBI, with Jake Sanders, have coordinated their efforts with the Governor's office, and on a particular day, a platoon from the national guard accompanied the

FBI when the appropriate arrests were made for all those on the Baldwin Bank Roll, which included the Mayor.

"In addition, to the corruption in the City Hall and the Police Departments, there was also a list of future short-term and long-term operations that the Baldwin Organization planned to carry out, which apparently really alarmed the FBI. As the additional information involved federal politics. So Jake and the FBI are now very busy monitoring numerous people. Numerous arrests were pending. I guess we will find out more from him."

Chapter 11

Release from the Hospital

While Chris was recuperating in Dr. James Adams's Clinic, Alycia, Allen, and Kiara again came to see him. Alycia always gave Chris a kiss on his cheek, and Kiara surprisingly always kissed him softly on his bruised lips. Chris was always happy to see them. Chris had already fallen in love with Kiara for some obvious reasons. There was something magical about her that Chris couldn't explain, but holding her hand or having her touching him gave him a warm and an amazing feeling of a kind of security. Chris just couldn't wait to see her again.

"Listen, folks, I really appreciate what you have done for me, and, Mr. Taylor, I really appreciate your Lawyer getting my name changed to Chris Canyon as well. Now Uncle Dwayne Baldwin will assume that his nephew, Eric Baldwin, is dead and gone out of his life. But little does he know."

Yes, his Uncle Dwayne, had stripped him totally financially and was now convinced that Eric Baldwin was history. That was in part true. Eric Baldwin was gone, but just like the Phoenix, out of the Ashes, Chris Canyon had now come back, almost from the dead, to take his place and to haunt Dwayne in the future and to ultimately bring him down.

Also, Chris Canyon still had several other debts to repay as well, in addition to the murder of his Mother and Father, but also for the murder of the innocent Olivia and the assault on his own back. And now his renewed attempt to kill him again, since the car bomb had not done its job, and had left Eric still alive. All that would wait till he returned from his Tour of Duty with the Navy SEALs.

"Listen, Chris, changing the subject, once Dr. Adams releases you from the clinic, and since we know that you have no place to go, we all were thinking that we have a bunkhouse-type facility at our Estate that caters to our few resident employees. Most all now live outside the Estate, so we really do need someone on the Estate basically as a guard-type character. The beds are all private, but all the other facilities are shared, and since we need another Assistant in our stables anyway, we were wondering if you'd like to come and work for us and live on the Estate?"

"Are you serious? God, that would be fantastic, yes, I owe you all so much all ready. Yes, I would love that. I'd do any kind of job that you asked me to. Thank you. God, you folks and Kiara, you really have been just fantastic."

So finally, after more than three weeks, almost a full month, in Dr. Adam's clinic, Chris Canyon was finally released.

*　　*　　*

At the Estate, Chris had settled into his new job, which was basically looking after the stalls of the top thoroughbreds being housed and trained by the Wind Crest Hills Thoroughbred Estate's top and experienced thoroughbred trainers. Chris was responsible in cleaning the stalls and for making sure that there was always enough water and food available for the horses and that the horses were well looked after and in a very calm, relaxed atmosphere.

The horses, being purebred thoroughbreds, all tended to be very high strung, and some were extremely sensitive to intrusions into their stalls and were very selective as to who could enter their stalls and who could not.

One horse, specifically a large black stallion called Midnight, a magnificent animal with an unbelievable pedigree, was super sensitive to intruders in his domain and frightened all the attendants that were assigned to look after the stalls.

After being shown what to do, Chris walked from one stall to the next one as he cleaned the horse's stalls, and at the same time, he made friends with the horses, talking to them quietly in a very quiet soothing voice, which the horses seemed to really like. Unbeknownst to Chris, he had a special touch and sound when he talked that really relaxed the horses and calmed them down. They felt no intrusion. In fact, they actually played with him. His gentleness and his handling of the horses was very unusual, and the horses all accepted him.

The last stall was Midnight's, the typically uncontrollable stallion who always terrorized anyone that came near him, but Chris, not knowing anything about Midnight, just walked into his stall in his calm, slow manner. Then he walked over to Midnight and stroked his nose and head and treated him to several sugar cubes and brushed his long mane. Then he actually wrapped his arms around Midnight's neck and hugged him, all the while softly talking to Midnight as if they were both friends. Amazingly Midnight was totally comfortable with Chris.

The Stalls' Manager, Bill was absolutely amazed at just how calm Midnight was acting. He immediately called Allen Taylor to see what was happening.

Midnight was totally relaxed, and he too played with Chris. He nudged Chris with his big head while Chris was cleaning his stall. Chris laughed softly and hugged him again. This was totally uncharacteristic of Midnight, but there was something about Chris obviously that Midnight sensed and liked; Chris was no threat to him. Chris was a friend.

When Allen arrived, he was simply amazed. Midnight was as calm as he had ever seen him. What magic did Chris have to pacify Midnight like this? No one else had been even able to enter his stall. This was really great. Perhaps with Chris's help, they could finally get Midnight out onto the track and start training him into the top thoroughbred racing horse he was born to be, according to his excellent pedigree.

As Midnight was his last stall, Chris took a brush and began to brush Midnight down. Midnight stood there quietly, turning his head and watching Chris brush him. When Chris was done, he offered Midnight some more water, which he drank comfortably and very peacefully. Midnight had found someone he was totally comfortable with.

When Alycia and Kiara arrived, they too watched in wonder. "God, he really has Midnight literally eating out of his hand. Amazing."

Chris, of course, had no idea that he was being watched.

Then when he was finished, he left Midnight in the stall. When he walked out, Midnight stuck his head out over the gate, and Chris hugged him again around the neck and talked to him quietly and soothingly.

"See you tomorrow, buddy," said Chris quietly.

Back in the shadows where Allen, Bill, Alycia, and Kiara were standing, Bill turned to Allen and said, "Mr. Taylor, he certainly has a really feel for the horses. They all accepted him into their stalls without any problems, but I was certainly surprised at Midnight's reaction. He really is the first person who has been able to connect with him. It really is amazing."

"Yes, it really is amazing. Perhaps Midnight would now allow us to train him. With Chris's help, it may be possible as Midnight has really accepted him almost unconditionally, which is really fantastic. I know Mr. Wainwright will be ecstatic, no doubt," said Allen with a smile.

Alycia and Kiara were astounded as well. Chris's ability to communicate with the horses and specifically with Midnight was absolutely great. There was something about Chris they just couldn't understand. He was unlike anyone any of them had met before.

Yet they had found him on the side of a deserted road, near death, but with their help and that of Dr. Adams, their family friend, this unknown kid had pulled through and survived.

Yet in many ways, this young man was someone special, unlike anyone they had met before. Both Kiara and Alycia quickly developed strong feelings for this young and handsome stranger. Kiara was especially infatuated by Chris, and every opportunity she had, she spent with him.

But Alycia too was really impressed by him, and strangely she too had strong feelings for him, especially after she and Kiara had seen him completely naked.

Chapter 12

The Peaceful, Serene Evening

One evening Kiara was looking around for Chris, as they were going to watch a movie together, but he never showed up.

"Where's Chris, Mom?" asked Kiara

"I think he's still cleaning up the stalls and stables. It's funny, but all the horses seem to like him, which is strange, but he really is able to calm them all down, especially Midnight, which really is amazing," said Alycia.

"You know he had his stitches out today as well, and the cast off his arm was also removed, so I assume he'll be able to play his guitar again. Boy, he really loves that guitar, and you know, Kiara, now that the bruises have virtually disappeared and the stitches are out, he is actually quite the handsome young man."

"Yes, I know, Mom!" said Kiara with a sly smile.

Alycia laughed. Yes, she knew Kiara was somewhat interested in the strange young man.

"And I think he has noticed his blonde Angel as well."

"I hope so," said Kiara, smiling, as she walked out to the stables, stopping at some of the stalls to stroke the heads of the various other thoroughbreds as well. They loved her soft caresses too. Suddenly she heard a guitar in the background, then unexpectedly, she heard someone singing, a familiar song she had heard a few years ago. The song was sung by the English entertainer Cliff Richard from one of his early movies, **Summer Holiday.** The song was called "The Next Time."

"God, it has to be Chris. He's the only one with a guitar, but I never knew he could sing or play the guitar so beautifully," she said to herself, as she made her way closer to where Chris was seated, which was right next to Midnight's stall.

Chris sat on a bale of hay beside Midnight's stall as he flexed his fingers, then he continued his melody. Midnight snorted a few times and shook his head. Chris laughed. "So you like the sound of the guitar, Midnight," said Chris with a smile.

Midnight shook his big head.

Then Chris restarted his song again as his fingers got used to moving up and down the frets of his guitar again. It felt good. He had missed it. Then softly he started to sing again.

They say I'll love again someday

A truer love will come my way, the
Next Time
But after you there'll never be a Next
Time for Me

Silently, Kiara who was really amazed at what she heard, found a place to sit on a pile of paving bricks, and she watched Chris from the shadows. Then unexpectedly Alycia slid down beside her.

"Hey, he never told us he could sing," she whispered with a smile as she hugged Kiara. So together they sat there listening to this impromptu concert as Chris continued his song.

They say that I'll find happiness
In someone else's warm caress, the Next
Time
I'll soon forget your kiss and heartaches
such as this
Will just be ancient history

Kiara looked at her mom and saw that she had closed her eyes and was enjoying the song too. Kiara was absolutely thrilled. Why hadn't he told her about his singing and guitar playing? This was such a surprise. Kiara just loved his soft gentle voice and his obvious talent on the guitar.

They say that I'm a fool to weep
That I won't go on loosing sleep, the
next time

> And someone else will mend the
> heart you've broken in two
> But how can I fall in love the next time?
> When I'm still so very much in love, with
> you

Kiara was really excited to find that Chris was so talented, and she was so happy to have him staying at their ranch, where she could see him each and every day. Yes, there was no doubt that she was infatuated by this now handsome youth, and she was sure she was falling in love with him as well.

> Oh...How can I fall in love the next time?
> When I'm still so very much in love with
> you
> With you.

When the song was over, Kiara raced over to where Chris was seated, and Alycia walked over as well.

"Oh, Chris, that was just so beautiful. Mom and I loved it. Do you know any other songs?" asked Kiara anxiously.

Chris smiled. He was happy that Kiara and Alycia had enjoyed his song. "Sure, Kiara, I know lots and lots of songs," responded Chris softly so as not to destroy the serene, quiet setting and disturb all the horses in their stalls watching them.

"Could you sing another song for us? I know we'd really like that."

Chris looked up at Alycia, who smiled and nodded her head.

"Sure, okay, Kiara, you know I'll sing for you anytime you want me to...anytime. All right, this one is a little more recent from the King, Elvis Presley's 'Mary in the Morning,' a beautiful ballad that I just love."

"Hey, I think we both remember that one," said Alycia with a smile, and Kiara nodded her head. Chris picked out the melody first, then he started to sing, strumming his guitar softly and singing softly. The song was really beautiful, and both Alycia and Kiara, of course, just loved Chris's rendition of the tune.

> Nothing's quite as Pretty as Kiara in the Morning
> When through the sleepy haze I see her lying there
> Soft as the rain that falls on summer flowers
> Warm as the sunlight shining on her pretty head

"Isn't he just amazing? God, we never knew he could sing and play the guitar like this," said Kiara softly to Alycia.

> When I awake, and see her there so close beside me
> I want to take her in my arms.
> The ache is there so deep inside me,

Alycia really loved the romantic setting, with all the horses listening to Chris's soothing voice and the romantic playing of his guitar. Yes, both mother and daughter were feeling strange feelings for this virtual stranger who unexpectedly arrived on their Estate.

> Nothing's quite as Pretty as Kiara in the morning
> Chasing the rainbow in her dreams so far away
> And when she turns to touch me, I kiss her fingers so softly
> And then my Kiara wakes to live and love again

Kiara was absolutely thrilled as Chris had insert her name into his song, but then again Fate had told her that a complete stranger would steal her heart. She was right again.

> And Kiara's there in summer days or stormy weather
> She doesn't care how right or wrong the love we share
> We share together

As Chris sang, Midnight leaned forward and actually nudged Chris softly with his nose. Chris smiled, then continued his song.

Nothing's quite as pretty as Kiara in the
evening
Kissed by the shade of night and star-
light in her hair
And as we walk, I hold her close beside
me
All our tomorrows for a lifetime we
will share.
Uh Ha.

After Chris finished the song, Kiara ran up to
him and wrapped her arms around him and passionately kissed him for a long time, as Alycia stood
by and smiled. Yes, Kiara loved him and had, surprisingly, right from the start.

Then Alycia walked up to Chris, and she too
smiled and said, "If Kiara can kiss you, then so can
I," and then she too wrapped her arms around
him and kissed Chris hard on his lips, and with
her tongue as well, which surprised Chris, but not
Kiara. Kiara just laughed. The fact was, mother
and daughter both loved Chris, and Chris was not
complaining.

"Just a little reward for the concert, Chris,"
said Alycia with a smile. Yes, both Kiara and Alycia
both appeared to have fallen for Chris in their own
ways.

Chris now knew he loved Kiara, but now he
saw Alycia in a different light as well after her
sweet unexpected kiss. Chris, for the first time, felt
warm. He was really thrilled with Kiara, and he
knew she would be his first real girlfriend and his

first real love. And he was also excited by Alycia's passionate French kiss as well.

Being kissed passionately by Kiara, Chris thought, was really great, as he already had fallen in love with her, but it was strange when Alycia also kissed him. It was very different kiss as Immediately Alycia had pushed her tongue into his mouth and explored his mouth with her long sexy tongue, providing him a most passionate kiss as well.

Kiara and Alycia just laughed, but Chris was somewhat confused. Girlfriends' Mothers don't usually kiss their daughters' boyfriends especially so passionately.

Also, the fact was that Alycia was a real hot MILF, with a perfect body for sex—large breasts, long legs, a nice protruding butt, long blonde hair, and a beautiful face, with full sensuous lips perfect for kissing and other sexual activities.

Neither Kiara or Alycia made anything of it, but they often came out to the stables when Chris played his guitar and sang some haunting ballads that both Kiara and Alycia loved.

One night Kiara was out there alone, as Alycia was busy with something. She listened to Chris singing again, and when Chris was finished, Kiara dragged him unexpectedly into an empty stall and quickly unbuckled his belt. She slid his jeans and underwear down and immediately took him into her mouth. This was the first oral act that she had had with Chris. It was her first. Chris certainly didn't resist at all, as he fondled her very ample soft naked breasts, which were now exposed as Kiara had pushed her tank top down for Chris's enjoyment.

While they were wrapped up in their sexual world, Alycia quietly snuck into the stall, and suddenly she knelt down beside Kiara with a great big smile on her face as she admired Chris's sizable member plunging in and out of Kiara's mouth.

"Oh my God!" uttered Kiara, totally shocked.

"Oh, D-damn!" stuttered Chris.

Quickly Alycia calmed them down. "Relax, you two, this is wonderful, I am so happy you have reached this stage in your relationship. I already know you both love each other, and stimulating each other sexual is very healthy, so please don't stop. I just love seeing you both so much into each other. However, perhaps I can give you a few pointers to make it more enjoyable for you both. You are already doing a fantastic job, but you'd be able to, do it better with a few tips," whispered Alycia.

"Okay, Mom," said Kiara softly, more relaxed by Alycia's attitude and her not being upset at all, but in fact, very supportive. "Show me."

The bewildered Chris watched silently as Kiara passed his member over to Alycia, who instantly engulfed it into her mouth and instantly proceeded giving Chris the full treatment.

After watching for a few minutes, Kiara wanted to continue where she left off. "Okay, Mom, I see what I need to do, thanks," said Kiara. She anxiously wanted to get Chris back in her mouth as she desperately wanted to experience Chris's first release in her mouth.

Alycia just smiled. She was happy for them both, as she obviously now loved both.

Chris was no virgin. The girls at his previous school had taught the Nashville Rebel all about teen-age love and sex, which he had certainly enjoyed. He had certainly enjoyed the variety of sensuous young ladies he had entertained at the drive-ins, and who had educated him in a variety of ways and techniques at their parties. However, he never had what one would call a steady girlfriend. The girls at school were happy to share him completely as they kept him secured with continual dates on all the weekends all through the school years.

The Nashville Rebel belonged to all the school's girls, and they all loved him and taught him all about teenage sex. Sometimes they entertained him with two or three girls simultaneously. Again, the Nashville Rebel did not complain.

At this point, neither Kiara nor Alycia had any idea that Chris was, in fact, the Nashville Rebel. Yes, Kiara had heard of him, but she had never heard him sing or seen him perform, even though he had had been on stage at her school several times. But each time he had been there, Kiara, for whatever reason, hadn't been there. Kiara, in turn, had told Alycia all about the Nashville Rebel, but neither had ever seen him perform, and neither had ever heard him sing before.

Thus, following that first night and after a spell, the soft slow ballads and the guitar solos performed by Chris became the norm after Chris had finished cleaning the stalls each night. The soothing sounds of his guitar playing and singing really relaxed the horses and excited Kiara, who was always now waiting for him in the shadows.

Each night after his dreamy ballads, Chris always met Kiara at Stall 18 for a night of passionate sex.

Typically, Kiara was out there listening to Chris's songs, and after the song was over, she made her way to Stall 18, which was only used to store bails of hay. On top of the bails was a relatively flat area the size of a king-size bed, where Kiara had dragged two large blankets and spread them out for her and Chris's pleasure and enjoyment. There in the shadows, they made love to each other virtually every night, especially whenever Allen was away, which was often. Yes, they really loved each other more than words could say. By this time Chris had introduced Kiara to anal sex as well, which Kiara really loved and looked forward to each night. Fate had provided them the direction, and now they were bonded together, and they loved it.

Alycia was well aware of their activity as Kiara snuck out each night to meet with Chris and to make passionate love to each other until dawn. Alycia supported them totally as she was so pleased that Chris and Kiara had found each other.

However, she was secretly jealous of Kiara as she too wanted her sensuous body to be ravished by Chris as well.

Alycia secretly also found opportunities to make out with Chris as well, while Kiara was in school and Allen and the other staff were away some-where. Before leaving the ranch house, Alycia always removed her bra so as to allow Chris to fondle her naked full breasts hidden behind her blouse, while they made out. On numerous occasions, Alycia was able to perform fellatio on Chris as well, much to his pleasure.

Chris, of course, had no reason to complain, as he too loved the attention, and frankly Alycia was a goddess in her own right, with an unbelievable body.

Chapter 13

The Two Love Affairs

Kiara, by now, was well aware that her loving mom, Alycia, also loved Chris and wanted to have him make love to her, just like Chris did with her each night.

Alycia acknowledged that there was something magical about Kiara's and Chris's connection, as it had been there right from the start of the day that She and Allen had found Chris/Eric on that deserted desolate roadside.

Yes, it was strange to see just how attached the two had become, and even in his beat-up condition, looking like hell, and not really knowing who he was, Kiara had been there for him, irrespective, holding his hand and supporting him quietly with soft caresses and soft, tender kisses, while they waited for the doctor to arrive.

Yes, it was almost magical. Whatever had Fate instilled in Kiara about this young man, only Kiara knew. The fact was, she stuck to Chris like glue, and Chris was just totally blown away by Kiara. She was without a doubt his one and only.

The strange part of this scenario was that Alycia, too, had been caught up in that same mysterious web, as she too developed strange, almost hungry feelings for this handsome youth, and she too lusted for him as well.

So, whenever Allen was out of town, when Kiara was in school and the Estate horse trainers were out on the various tracks and paddocks, Alycia sought out Chris and introduced him to her glorious naked voluptuous breasts, as they made out, passionately hidden in the vacant stalls during the day. When there was time, Alycia even performed fellatio on Chris, much to his pleasure, but they hadn't made love to each other as yet. Chris, in his own way, adored Alycia and her voluptuous body, but his heart belonged to Kiara, without a doubt. Strangely Kiara's body too had developed into the voluptuous duplicate of Alycia's body, with all the curves all in the same place. Their breasts were virtually identical, it was quite amazing, and Chris in his own way wasn't complaining, but Kiara was his true love.

Alycia dreamt of being completely ravished by Chris, her performing fellatio on Chris, and him performing cunnilingus on her in the 69 position, and then the penetration and their nightlong sex-capade.

Yes, she dreamt!

Kiara saw that and knew that her mother Alycia had passionate feelings for Chris just like she did, but it didn't concern her, and in fact, she found it quite natural.

Kiara knew, irrespective, that she and Chris were now one, and that her mother couldn't change that in any way, and she wouldn't have wanted to anyway, but undeniably the lust in Alycia's sensuous body ached or desired to be taken by this handsome young youth!

Yes, unexpectedly two romances developed in the Estate, one with Kiara, who had fallen in love with Chris or Eric right from the start, just as fate had determined; however, suddenly there was also Alycia, being left alone far too often, by Allen with all his business trips and commitments. Alycia felt a strange hunger developing, yes, a strange stir deep within in her sensuous body for this young man who had arrived in their Estate so unexpectedly.

The fact was that Alycia and Kiara were very close and slept together often when Allen was away on business. They enjoyed each other's soft sensuous bodies and their loving lesbian-type nights together.

Unbeknownst to Alycia, Kiara saw the lust and love mixed together in Alycia's eyes for Chris and smiled. Kiara knew that Chris was hers, but she and Alycia were close too, and Kiara had no problem with sharing Chris with her gorgeous sex-starved Mother. In fact, she had already planned a three-way trip to the constellations on graduation night, which no one knew about at this stage. Alycia had confirmed to her that she had reserved the Master Bedroom for Kiara and Chris while Allen was away again.

"Listen, Mom, I know you love Chris too, I can see it in your eyes, and don't bother denying it, I know, so I have resolved that on Graduation Night, we should celebrate the Graduation with a three-way session in the Master Bedroom, I know Chris wouldn't mind, and I'm sure he too has strong feelings for you as well. We'll have a wild night ravishing each other right until dawn. Besides, by that time you will have already had sex with him, you know it will be great!"

"What do you mean I will have had sex with him already, Kiara?"

Kiara just laughed. "Look, tomorrow night, we are having a girls' sleepover at Bonnie's place with June, Krystal, Bonnie, and me, and I'll be spending the night with my girlfriends, so I'll need you to do me a favour," said Kiara with a sly smile.

"Yeah, okay, what is it?" inquired Alycia.

"Well, as you already know, I meet Chris at stall 18 every night, and we make love until dawn, whenever Dad's away, so as I am going to be tied up with the girls tomorrow night and Dad is away, I want you to stand in for me for the night and let Chris ravish your sensational body, like I know you would want him to do."

"What? Are you serious? You want Chris, your boyfriend, to make love to me, tomorrow night, like he does to you?"

"Precisely." Kiara smiled.

"Does Chris know what you are planning?"

"Of course, not. Let's surprise him...Hey, Mom, I know deep down you really want to, and I know it would be a great surprise for Chris to find you there all naked under the blankets, instead of me."

"What if he refuses?"

"Are you kidding? He won't. I know it. He has always acknowledged just how beautiful and voluptuous you are, and how your 38" breasts stand without any sagging at all, so when he realizes it's okay with me, he'll be only to happy to ravish you all night long, you'll see! Do it, Mom."

"Listen, Darling, are you sure you want me to have passionate sex with your boyfriend?"

"Hey, Mom, look I love you both, and I have been thinking about us having a three-way together. I was thinking about our Graduation Night. But first things first, he needs to do you good before that. I think that would be great. You deserve some hot passionate sex, and Chris will give it to you, for sure. Look, I have no problem with Chris making passionate love to you. I think he would love to do just that, and indirectly having you seduce him with your voluptuous naked body, how could he refuse?

"Look, Mom, I guarantee you will not regret it. Besides, he is really fantastic. He knows just how to turn me on and inside out, and you already know he has the credentials to take you into outer space, and the way you have kissed him before, he knows that your body wants him. God Mom, you'll love it without a doubt."

"Okay, Hun, you've convinced me, I'll take your place tonight. God Just thinking about it, has made me hot already."

Kiara laughed. Alycia really didn't know what a night she would have or what to expect. "Yes, I know, but are you sure you want me to do this, Kiara, on your Graduation Night as well? After all, this is your special night. You don't want me spoiling it for you."

"Hey, Mom, I would love to see Chris buried deep inside you. It will be a real turn-on for me. Rest assured, with his stamina and his expertise, he will really give us both a night to remember, while he is away. Then when he gets back, we'll do it all over again, which will be sensational. You'll see. But first things first."

So the stage for that night's unexpected encounter between Alycia and Chris was set.

That night, Kiara joined her girlfriends for a passionate night of lesbian-type sex at Bonnie's place.

Meanwhile, back at the Estate, and with Allen away on business in Los Angeles, Alycia silently made her way into the stalls pavilion where Chris always sang one of his songs to his horses. Alycia silently climbed up the bails of hay to where Kiara had set up their nightly lovemaking sessions. Then in the shadows Alycia stripped completely and climbed naked under the blanket and patiently waited for Chris to show up.

Shortly after the song faded in the background, Alycia knew this was it. Chris would soon be there.

Alycia was anxious to see Chris's reaction when he saw the luscious naked Alycia there waiting for him instead of his Kiara.

Finally, when Chris arrived, he too quickly stripped ready for action, as he usually did. Slowly Alycia lowered the blanket, exposed her full pair of 38s glowing in the low light of the loft. Alycia smiled as she saw that Chris was already aroused totally. Yes, her night of sensuous passion was about to begin.

"Alycia, what are you doing here? Where's Kiara?" said Chris, somewhat surprised.

"She couldn't make it tonight!" said Alycia with a smile.

"God, you look fantastic, Alycia."

"She's at her a girlfriend's sleep over tonight, and she asked me to stand in for her," said Alycia seductively as she showed off her full breasts, offering them to him.

"Did she really?"

"Yes, lover, she did!"

"Well, I guess we mustn't disappoint her," said Chris with a smile, more aroused than ever, as he slowly pulled the blanket away, exposing Alycia full luscious naked figure. "Is this going to be the long version or the short one?"

"Oh, baby, let's make it the long, long, long version. I want us to do everything, leaving nothing out. Take me to outer space, Baby, take me, Baby, Take me."

Instantly Chris was between her legs performing cunnilingus hungrily on her as his hands fondled both her full breasts enthusiastically. Alycia didn't even have time to get ready as Chris instantly took her away. Quickly Chris brought her to her first orgasm, then without stopping, he just continued to the next one and then a third one. Alycia was already floating on a cloud. Kiara was right, Chris knew what to do. No one had done this to Alycia before. Now she knew she was having a night she would never forget, as Chris took control of her body.

Suddenly with her legs on his shoulders, Chris slowly penetrated Alycia. She held her breath until he bottomed out at her cervix, and then with one final powerful thrust, he was inside her womb. Alycia was totally beside herself. Never had sex been like this. No wonder Kiara always looked like she had been in a passionate session with Chris. Now she was having the same treatment herself, and she loved it.

"God, this is the best sex ever," she panted as she held her legs up in the air as Chris pounded her with his powerful thrusts. The amorous assault on Alycia continued as they moved into different positions throughout the night. Chris even introduced Alycia to anal sex as he provided her with the complete spectrum of sexual acts.

Alycia was totally out in left field. Never had sex been so intense. She was convinced she was already in paradise. She had never experience anything like this before in her life. Her body was so alive, so aroused, and she was so thrilled that Kiara had asked her to stand in for her. Chris had pounded her powerfully, deeply giving her sensations she had never experienced before.

Now she realized why Kiara was so wrapped up in Chris. The fact was, he delivered, and Kiara loved it, obviously.

Just before the sun came up, Alycia dragged her ravished body back to the ranch house, ran herself a hot bubble bath, and quietly slipped into the warmth of the warm soothing water.

"Aaah," she sighed. "That was the ultimate. God, I never knew it could be like this!"

She had never been loved so passionately, so thoroughly, so completely without any breaks. Her body was still so alive with sensations and feelings she had never experienced before. Chris had used her whole body with no exceptions and ravished her in every possible way. Alycia could not believe what Chris had done to her. This was something she had never experienced before, and she had loved very minute, every second of his Amorous Assault.

She felt as if she was transported into another world and hoped that the assault would never end. It had been pure ecstasy.

Kiara had been absolutely right. Chris knew what he was doing. and he had all the necessary attributes to pleasure her beyond belief. Alycia had lost count of all her orgasms and the times she took Chris's gifts in her mouth.

Yes, it was a night she knew she would never forget!

* * *

The next day Kiara approached Alycia. "How did it go last night, Mom?"

"Oh God, Kiara, it was just unbelievable, I have never had such exciting sex in my whole life, God it was just fantastic."

"I told you he was different, and I knew he would make love to you like you had never had before."

"You, Darling, were absolutely right. Oh God, I'm still floating on air, even now."

Kiara laughed softly. She knew what Chris would do to her, and he obviously had taken her completely.

"Okay, Darling, now I know I can't wait for you two to come back from the dance. But as you said, first things first. Oh, Kiara, thank you for including me in in this."

Chapter 14

The Graduation Dance: The Nashville Rebel

With the school year ending and with Kiara graduating from high school, and soon heading off to Alabama University to study to become a Doctor, there was still one big party to attend. The Graduation Prom—that was the highlight of the year, the school's graduation night dance. However, at this point, Kiara did not have a date for the dance.

Being as beautiful as she was, yes, she was in high demand at school; all the guys wanted to date her and to have a chance to entertain her royally through the night, but she had rejected all numerous requests by other boys, as she had her own plans. Yes, so she was without a date for the prom, the school's graduation dance.

So, unfazed, after school one afternoon Kiara raced around the stalls to find Chris again as he was cleaning up again. She was on a mission!

As soon as she saw him, she raced up and kissed him passionately, as she now did often. "Hey, Chris, our school is having its Prom, the school's graduation dance, next week on Saturday night, and I was really hoping that you'd be well enough so you could take me," said Kiara with her cute smile. "I would really, really love for you to be my date for the special night!"

"Are you kidding? Of course, Kiara! I'd be proud and absolutely honored to go as your date, but if you would rather, you know, I could come as your steady boyfriend. Would that be better?" inquired Chris with a smile. "I would just love to have you as my official Steady Girlfriend."

"Oh God, are you kidding? Oh yeah, Chris, I would love to be your Steady Girlfriend. For sure, you've just made my day, and as my steady boyfriend, you realize you can kiss me now anytime you want." She laughed happily. She wrapped her arms around him and kissed him passionately again.

Alycia knew the night of the graduation dance was typically an all-night affair and that many couples just rented hotel rooms so they could make love to each other privately.

Alycia was well aware that Kiara and Chris had been now dating for quite some time and that they both obviously were very much in love with each other. She also knew they had made love to each other regularly. She had no problem with that, and in fact, she supported their Love Affair completely. The fact was Kiara and Chris had been making love to each other like rabbits at every opportunity they had, virtually every night in one of the vacant stalls on a large blanket over the stacked bails of straw/hay.

On graduation night, Kiara had bought some erotic, sexy yellow-and-silver lingerie to excite Chris and to really turn him on for their journey to the constellations, but with her Dad away, Kiara had second thoughts and decided that they should have a three-way trip to the constellations with Alycia included.

Also, as Chris was leaving soon to join the Navy SEALs program and Kiara was headed to Alabama University to study medicine, they would be separated for at least three years, so Alycia made a suggestion to Kiara.

"Listen, Darling, as Dad is away and as this really is one of the few times you two will be together, I have reserved our Master Bedroom for you two tonight, and that is for all night."

"Oh God, that is fantastic. I guess you know that we love each other and have for quite some time, and now after graduation, we will both be headed in different directions, but we have vowed that our Love Affair is not over and that we will continue where we left of when we arrive back home. It is not going to be easy being separated for so long, but we know we have something special and that we will be able to catch up when we get back.

"Oh, Mum, tonight is really going to be so special, and to be locked in each other arms as we head up to the stars will be so wonderful and something we both know we will never forget."

*   *   *

At the Graduation Dance, after Kiara and Chris had made the scene and Kiara had proudly introduced Chris, her steady boyfriend, to all her girlfriends, they all enjoyed the dance, with Larry Fleming, the lead singer of the Viscounts, a local band, was putting on a good show.

After the end of his first set, Larry noticed Chris several times dancing with the ever-gorgeous Kiara. He thought he recognized him but wasn't sure. Finally, Larry approached him and led him away from the others. "Listen, friend, I think I know you, don't I?" said Larry.

"Hey, Larry, you sure do, but it's Chris Canyon now, don't ask why, but the rest is still the same."

"As a favor, would you do us a couple of your songs for your fans?" Larry laughed. "For old times' sake. We've missed you at our school's sock hops and dances. You can use my guitar."

"Sure, Larry, be my pleasure," responded Chris with a smile.

So, when Larry Fleming finished his set, he immediately spoke to the audience. "Hey, folks, I hope you are all having fun tonight. Hey, listen, I think I have a surprise for you all. Out of curiosity, has anyone heard of our own Lexington's Nashville Rebel ?"

Suddenly there were loud screams, as all the girls acknowledged knowing their local teenage idol.

"Well, folks, quite by accident, I have just discovered our very own Nashville Rebel is, in fact, here at our dance tonight, incognito if you will, as our Kiara Taylor's new steady boyfriend."

Kiara immediately looked at Chris, who was just smiling innocently.

"And hey, if we all could encourage him a little, perhaps we could get him to come up on stage a sing several songs for us. What do you say?"

The screams were unanimous.

"We want the Nashville Rebel!" shouted everyone.

Kiara was flabbergasted. She had no idea that her boyfriend Chris was actually the Nashville Rebel. Yes, she had heard of him but had never seen him perform or sing before.

Chris just smiled as he kissed Kiara. "Excuse me for a few moments," said Chris.

"Oh my God, you never told me you were the Nashville Rebel," said Kiara, all excited.

"You never asked," responded Chris with a smile. Kiara jabbed him playfully.

So Chris made his way up onto the stage, borrowed Larry's guitar, and walked calmly up to the microphone. He looked around at the excited audience, and then he saw Kiara with a giant grin on her face.

"Thank you very much, and my sincere best wishes to all the grads here tonight." Then instantly as his hand came down on his guitar, he broke into his signature song, Waylon Jennings's "Nashville Rebel." The Viscounts knew these songs and just joined in as well.

> They call me The Nashville Rebel
> They said leave that boy Alone
> Don't Give him Advice, or he'll turn to ice
> And you might as well talk to Stone
> But I've got things to Do, things to say
> In my own way...

As Chris was singing, Kiara was really beside herself. God, she couldn't believe it. All her girl-friends and their dates all crowded around her as they watched their own teenage idol rockin' and boppin' on stage, entertaining everyone. All the dancing had stopped as everyone crowded around the stage.

As soon as the first song was over, with every girl and most of the guys screaming for more, Chris switched to an early Elvis classic, "Baby Let's Play House."

> Oh Baby baby baby, ooh baby baby baby
> Come back baby I wanta play house with you
> Well, you may go to college, you may go to school
> You may have a pink Cadillac
> But don't you be nobody's fool

Now baby, come back baby, come
Come back baby, come
I wanna place house with you
Now listen. And I'll tell you baby,
What I talking about
Come on back, to me little girl
So we can play a little house,
and we can neck like we did before
I wanna play house with you.

Chris, just like Elvis had done, gyrated around the stage too, which excited all the girls. Yes, the dancing had all stopped as all the teenagers gathered around the stage to watch their own teenage idol. Their own Nashville Rebel was setting the night on fire. The Teens loved him, and they just loved his version of the song.

Next came Johnny Restivo's "The Shape I'm In." These were some old rock 'n' roll classics, so the Viscounts joined in backing the Nashville Rebel.

I can't go, I can't stay
It's your fault, I'm this way
I ain't ever been, hmmm, the shape I'm
in
I can't sit, I can't stand
This feeling is so grand
Hoping it never ends, hmmm, the
shape I'm in

Chris looked down at the happy, excited Kiara and blew her a kiss as he danced around on the stage to his music. The band played along as Larry clapped his hands enthusiastically on the sidelines.

> You tell me no, then you tell me yes
> You keep my mind a wreck
> I'm not gonna ever rest, I'm gonna get you, yeah
> I feel good, I feel bad
> I feel happy, I feel sad
> But I love you all over again
> I love being in the shape I'm in.
> Hmmm, yeah...the shape I'm in.

After the applause, Chris spoke again. "This next song I wrote myself about the time I fell in love with Kiara not so long ago. I hope you, all like it. It's called 'Your Wonderland.'" He immediately picked out the basic melody on the guitar.

> "What do you think?" The applause and screams followed.
> "Well, okay, here are some of the words..."
> And now, walking through your wonderland
> Holding on to each other's hands
> Walking through your wonderland
> Each night when your holding me so tight
> Give me kisses just right
> Walking through your wonderland.

Chris looked down and saw the smile on Kiara's happy face and saw her mouth form the words "I love you," which really warmed Chris's heart.

Yes, he had found his Angel. Before he went into his final song, Chris stopped for another minute and stood in front of the microphone, "Hey, you all, thank you so very much. It is so nice to be remembered. Thank you all. This last song is a one by an English entertainer called Billy Fury, and the song is called 'Once upon a Dream.' I am dedicating this song to my beautiful girlfriend, My Angel, My Everything, Kiara Taylor. I love you, Hun."

Then he immediately started his song on his guitar.

> Once, once upon a dream I met her
> Long ago but somehow, I can't forget her
> I met her, once upon a dream
> We built a castle where we planned to live together
> Precious moments in the land of never
> I met her once upon a dream

Suddenly the large gymnasium was silent as Chris's voice filled the large enclosure and all the teens swayed to the sensual lyrics and melody. It was a song no one had heard before in the United States, and it silenced the crowded hall. Chris just smiled as he continued his song. Kiara was lost in their own world. She loved this Nashville Rebel, and she had from the start.

Dreams can come true Darling
That's what they say
Prove that you're real
And its my lucky day
Once, once, upon a dream I met her
Never, never thought we'd be
together, forever
Riding on our dreams
I met her, once, upon a dream
I met her, once, upon a dream

The noise of the screams and applause was deafening. Yes, the Nashville Rebel was still their own idol, and they all adored him. But there was that beautiful young blonde Angel standing on the dance floor with her girlfriends and their applicable dates. Kiara's eyes were full of tears of joy. Yes, she really did love him. Her boyfriend was just amazing.

Larry was back on stage. "Chris, that was fantastic! Thank you so much, my friend. Looks like everyone still loves you, Buddy. Our own Nashville Rebel!"

Unbeknownst to Chris, Larry had recorded the Nashville Rebel's entire performance, including Billy Fury's hit song "Once upon a Dream."

For Kiara, that Saturday Night Dance had been the best. It would live forever in her dreams, the night that her boyfriend, the Nashville Rebel, the local teenage idol, had acknowledged his love for her in front of all her girlfriends and school friends.

Yes, she was so thrilled to be spoken for and by Lexington's own teenage idol, the Nashville Rebel.

Next, after all the voting was tabulated, Kiara was nominated as the Queen of the Graduation Dance, and with the Nashville Rebel as her date, they were certainly the couple of the Graduation Dance. Kiara really couldn't believe it. It certainly was a night she would never forget, that was for sure. Their photographs would fill their yearbook, and the unexpected appearance of the Nashville Rebel, her actual boyfriend, at the Graduation Dance was really exciting for Kiara.

This time the advantage was that Chris Canyon looked nothing like the scrawny Eric Baldwin, so no one actually recognised his original persona. Seeing the new handsome Nashville Rebel, the old version was quickly forgotten.

After the grad dance, Kiara and Chris joined a group of Kiara's girlfriends and their dates at one of the local restaurants for a superb dinner. All her girlfriends were super impressed to have their grad dinner in the company of the Nashville Rebel and his girlfriend, Kiara Taylor. Kiara was so thrilled as she really became the center of attraction, being the girlfriend of their local celebrity.

After the dinner, Kiara suggested that Chris actual give the girls a soft, tender kiss on their lips as a special treat.

"Congratulations, Ladies, on your graduation. It has been a pleasure meeting you all, and I wish you all the best in your futures," said Chris as he gave them all the farewell kiss, which Kiara's girl-friends thought was really cool.

Kiara was now more than anxious to return home as she and Chris had the luxury of Alycia's Master Bedroom for their all-night sexual session. Yes, this was the night they were going to take their Flight to the Constellations, and it was going to last all night. Kiara just couldn't wait, but she had other plans as well.

"Thank you, baby, for making my graduation dance night so super special. I'll never forget it, especially with the appearance of the Nashville Rebel. Tonight, baby, I'm so looking forward to our night in the Master Bedroom. I'm gonna show you just how much I love you, and then you'll never want anyone else but me. I know you've already taken my virginity, but tonight in a soft comfortable bed will really be sensational for all of us." In her anxiety, she let it slip, but Chris didn't pick up the "us" part.

Then in the parking lot, which by this time was empty, and their car was virtually hidden under the shade of several large oak trees, Kiara couldn't wait any longer. There was this urgency in her for them to be joined.

"Oh Chris, my Darling, I am so turned on after all that has happened tonight. I really need you deep inside me right here and now." She unzipped Chris. Instantly, she pulled his pants and under-wear down to his knees and immediately took him in her mouth to get him ready. A minute later, with her sexy yellow thong in Chris's jacket pocket, her dress hiked up, Chris slipped into her, pene-trating her deeply as Kiara moaned softly. She just loved sex, and the more, the better. Yes, they were one again, locked together in their passion.

*   *   *

Back at the ranch, Kiara couldn't wait to tell her mom all that had happened on her special night.

Once she and Chris returned home, the excited Kiara immediately told Alycia all about their unbelievable night, which was far from over.

"Mom, you won't believe what happened tonight! Do you realize this guy here," said Kiara, killing herself laughing as she jabbed Chris again playfully, "yes, this guy! This guy is actually Lexington's teenage idol, The Nashville Rebel!"

"No kidding?" said Alycia, totally shocked but not surprised. "Is he really? I guess it is no wonder he knows all those beautiful songs and knows how to play that guitar like that." Alycia laughed. "So now the secret is out!"

"Yes, and the local band leader recognized him and had him go up on the stage and had him sing some songs. God, Mom, I couldn't believe it. Everybody stopped dancing just to watch him perform. Then the last song was a beautiful ballad, and he dedicated it to me and told everyone he loved me. I just about fainted. It really was unreal. God, I felt so special. And all the time, this here guy, all he did was smile," said Kiara as she clung to Chris, and Chris held her tight.

"God, Chris. God, I love you, Baby."

Kiara, knowing how Alycia felt about Chris as well, had an alternate plan for the three of them. Yes, it was going to be a three-way up journey to the constellations as Kiara and Alycia took Chris to heaven in a nightlong sexual extravaganza. And thus, Chris made passionate love to both of his lovers, in every which way, switching and penetrating his two partners, mother and daughter, continually all night long. It was sheer ecstasy for all three of them. A night that none of them would ever forget.

It was a Night in Paradise.

Chapter 15

The Night of Passion: The Three-Way

"Oh, Chris, Dad's away for a week up in New York at a convention, so Mom has vacated their master bedroom for us for the whole night, so we will be able to travel to the constellations and ravish and love each other like we haven't done before. God, it is going to be great being able to love each other on a soft, comfortable bed like that." Kiara laughed. "Is that okay with you, baby?"

The real fact was, Kiara and Chris had explored each other's bodies very thoroughly by this time, and they had spent many afternoons in deserted locations, ravishing each other endlessly. Oh yeah, they just loved sex and plenty of it. The drive-ins were all about sex, certainly not the movies, and Alycia had already guessed that. Even though Kiara always made a point to always comb her hair before returning home. Alycia, in her own way, coordinated with Kiara and never asked anything about the movies that had been playing as she knew neither Kiara or Chris would know anything about them, as they had other interests to deal with.

Chris was also grateful to the young and sex-starved ladies from his previous high schools where he graduated in sex education, thanks to the vivacious Jackie and the Young Ladies Social Club. Yes, he was well educated, and Kiara was benefitting from his vast experiences.

"Hey, Kiara, as long as I have you, everything is perfect. I have never loved anyone like I love you," whispered Chris.

"Thank you, Baby. God, you know I'm gonna really miss you so, but I'll be in college for three years, and you'll be gone to the Navy SEAL training for two years and then a one year active duty. When we get back, we'll never be apart again, I promise you that, and we'll probably be in bed for the first month catching up on all the loving we are going to be missing while we are apart, but we will catch up quickly, baby. We will. I know we will," said Kiara, her eyes sparkling like diamonds.

"Darling, from the first time I saw you, even in your beaten-up condition, fate told me you were going to be my boyfriend, my lover, and ultimately my lifetime mate—my husband. And I really believed her. From the first time I held your hand, I knew it was true. That is why you survived that accident. Fate had promised you for me."

"Kiara, rest assured I have never met anyone like you, and yes, we are going to lustfully ravish each other's bodies all night long, and we will be doing everything that a horny male and two raunchy females can dream up, including anal. Nothing will be left out. Oh yeah, the three of us will not forget tonight, that is for sure.

"Tonight, we will make passionate love to each other for the rest of the night. And once I get back from college and you return from your adventures with the Navy SEALS, we will do this all over again, just the three of us, and nobody will ever know. Then after that we will discuss our ongoing love affair and our actual union. Are you okay with that, Chris? Mom?"

"God, how could I refuse? This will be great."

"Kiara, from the day that Alycia and your dad found me, and when you walked into that room, I knew I had entered heaven, and the only place I am in heaven is wrapped up in your arms, so ultimately, you and I will be one again," said Chris as he took Kiara in his arms and kissed her passionately.

"Baby, I'll always be yours, and I will always love you. You know that now. Besides, we are already one," said Kiara with her special cute smile.

"Yes, we are, Baby, yes, we are!"

Chapter 16

The Three-Year Separation

The next morning after their visit to the Vulpecula Constellation, all three collapsed from total exhaustion just as the sun began to rise. Their night of sexual bliss had come to an end, and Alycia, Kiara, and Chris couldn't have been happier.

Now there would be three years of separation as Chris headed for the naval academy to enter the Navy SEALs training program and some active service upon completion of the two-year course. Chris had already prepared himself with some martial arts training in karate and tae kwon do, so even though he wasn't muscle bound now, he knew a new individual would return to Kentucky after his three grueling years of training and service. Yes, he would be a completely new man.

Kiara was now all prepared to attend Alabama University in their medical program. She was intent on becoming a doctor, and nothing was going to deter her from her plans. Now she knew that Chris would be back to claim his prize after the three years just as Fate had already primed them.

Yes, they both acknowledged there would be some romances and affairs during those three years, but all would be meaningless, and they were only there to fill the temporary gaps in their lives. Their hearts were already promised to each other, so any other relationships with other men or women would only be temporary meaningless entertainment and would bear no consequences on their existing relationship.

Even Alycia was all ready for the return of her daughter and the Nashville Rebel, and she was already anticipating their next journey as a three-some to the constellations above. However, she too had three years to kill.

And so Kiara headed for the University of Alabama, and Chris headed to Indianapolis, to the Naval Academy for his initial training.

All three knew that this three-way romance would continue upon Kiara's and Chris's returns. Fate had brainwashed them to believing that their love affair was on solid foundation and their love for each other would still be there when they returned.

Chapter 17

The Lost Three Years

Was it coincidental that Chris's three-year stint with the US Navy SEALs, two-year training program, and the additional year of active service and operational duty coincided with Kiara's medical course at the Alabama University, before she achieved her basic training to become a doctor? Yes, she would need a year of active experience, usually in the ER at some local hospital, before she could call herself a doctor. However, that basic on-site training and experience, she knew she could do that right in Lexington.

Then once Chris had served his three years and achieved the status of Navy SEAL Operative and Kiara had achieved her status as a Doctor, they could be together again, this time permanently, and to visit the constellations nightly as a couple or as a threesome with Alycia whenever the opportunity came up.

However, without it ever being said or discussed, they both knew that three years was a long time. There would be temporary miscellaneous dates, affairs and one-night stands and meaningless sex to fill the three-year gap for them both, but if their love was true and basically sanctioned by Fate, they would return home after the three years to continue where they had left off, plain and simple. The activities during those three years would be just fading memories.

Those were the unconfirmed plans for both of them, and after the three years, all that had happened during their three-year separation would be irrelevant and would be forgotten by both, never to be discussed or talked about in their future. Whatever happened would really be meaningless activities that really didn't affect their ultimate future happiness and would be forgotten, or so they, at least both thought.

They also realized that they could not just sit there for three years and hibernate and not enjoy some male or female companionships. They both accepted that there would be irrelevant relationships while they were apart. They fully believed that after three years, they would be back together again to continue where they left of on their magical love affair.

However, in a young adult's life, three years is an eternity! Anything could happen, whether they wanted it to or not!

So, facing reality, they knew they would just have to wait and see and keep their fingers crossed.

Chris Canyon

For Chris, the first part of the training was very intense, and there was very little time to socialize, which was what he had expected. But there were times for relaxing and social activities.

Near the academy, there was a variety of bars that provided, snacks, dinners, drinks, dancing, and some social activity catering to the SEAL recruits. So whenever they had some free time, that was where they all usually headed, to meet some local talent.

When Chris did have the opportunity to go out to these local bars, and when he did meet some cute college girls, he really wasn't looking for any long-term relationships or commitments, but occasionally he did hook up with some cute young ladies—blondes, brunette, or redheads, it really didn't matter—and he did indulge in various one-night stands.

But even as he was making love to them, his mind was elsewhere, so he never ever got too involved with any of them. Yes, they too were beautiful, yes, it was sex, and Chris really enjoyed the physical interaction, but he knew mentally it was temporary, nothing more. Yes, several dates were repeat dates, but the young ladies weren't stupid either. As soon as they realized that his heart just was not into their relationships, even though they really liked him and his soft gentle manner, they too subsequently just moved on and went looking for someone else, realizing there was no future with him.

Then surprisingly, one night, things got a little interesting when "she" walked in the door.

Kimiko Katherina Zemanova

Yes, one special night Kimiko Katherina Zemanova walked in through the door, looked around as if she was searching for someone, then suddenly she saw "him," yes, that really good-looking, solitary guy with long hair and an athlete's physique that she was looking for. Yes, he was there and alone. That vision unexpectedly did something to her. Just by chance he was sitting all by himself, without any girlfriend in sight, and the table had been set for a single person, which was perfect. Was this the guy Fate had told her about? Was this her lucky day? She hoped so!

Kimiko was an exceptionally beautiful eighteen-year-old black-haired Oriental beauty, heaven sent, the likes of which Chris had not seen, or could even have imagined, before. She was absolutely stunning. Chris could not take his eyes off her.

Her silky straight black hair hung down to her waist. Her figure was slightly on the slim side, but with a firm full bust and all her curves all in the right places. She looked simply amazing! She was dressed in a black silky fabric accentuated with Oriental motifs that looked like it had been just poured over her. It certainly highlighted all her sensuous curves.

Without a doubt, she looked so damned gorgeous, a real living doll. On her delicate feet, she wore black suede thin-strapped stiletto shoes that really excited Chris. Chris was impressed seeing her bare feet like that and was really excited. She smiled as she quickly made her way over to Chris as if she already knew him.

Her cute smile was irresistible. Chris was really turned on and anxious to find out where this mysterious gorgeous young lady had come from. Who was she?

Then the erotic fragrance of her perfume, Yves Saint Laurent's Opium, hit his brain, and he knew he had lost all control; he was hooked. Yes, she was now in total control.

"I'm sorry I'm late, Darling, but got stuck in the traffic," she purred as she leaned over and kissed Chris firmly on the lips, then licking the side of his face erotically. As she leaned over to him, her hand came to rest right on his privates. She squeezed him gently and smiled.

Chris couldn't believe what was happening. Was he really in an erotic dream or what? He was being seduced, and he knew it!

"I'll be right back, Hun. Just going to the Ladies' Room. Order me my usual glass of Chardonnay, will you please, Darling?" Then with another kiss, she disappeared.

Chris sat there dumbfounded. Who in the hell was she? But he acknowledged that she was absolutely gorgeous! He certainly couldn't deny that. Her face was just exquisite, with her slanted

Oriental eyes oh-so-sexily made up in purple tones and black eyeliner. Her full sensuous glossy purple-coloured lips just begging to be kissed and her special erotic smile set Chris's blood really boiling.

Without any hesitation, Chris quickly ordered the glass of Chardonnay for the mysterious young lady. Yes, she had taken control of the evening. Chris certainly was not complaining. He looked forward to seeing her again.

Suddenly, she reappeared from the ladies' restroom and almost floated over to where Chris was seated.

"Hi, Baby, it's so good to see you here." Without any hesitation, she took a sip of the Chardonnay. Then unexpectedly she again wrapped her arms around Chris and French kissed him passionately, allowing some of the wine in her mouth to flow into his mouth. He loved it. Unexpectedly the kiss lasted quite a long time, much longer than she or he had expected.

"Oh, wow, God! Where did you come from? Wow, kissing you is really sooo nice, Darling, so much more than I had hoped for," she said with a smile that really warmed Chris's heart. Wow!

Chris just smiled. Yes, the kiss was really delightful, and it really turned Chris on.

"You're one of the SEALs in training, I assume?"

"Yeah," responded Chris simply.

"So you'll be here for the next two years or so?"

"Yeah, I expect so."

"Well, wonderful. Just for you information, Baby, as of today, you belong to me. Yes, I will look after you for the next two years, basically until you leave. Also, when I say I will look after you, please understand—I will be your passionate lover every minute of the day and night that you are free and available. You will make love to me and penetrate me at every opportunity. You will make love to me day and night, wherever and whenever we can. You will explore every square inch of my sensuous body, and I will do the same with your body as well. And you will learn just how to turn me inside out, okay?"

"Perfect!" sighed Chris, totally overwhelmed by this exotic beauty.

"I have my own condo in town, so we won't be disturbed. I also have a new Corvette to get around in, so we'll have no need for taxis. Are you okay with all that, Baby?"

"Perfectly, but—"

Her fingers touched his lips to stop him from saying anything. She smiled and leaned over and kissed him softly, teasingly on his lips again. "Shhh...I know you are dying to know just who I am, but be fair, I don't know who you are either," she said with a smile as her hand squeezed his privates again. "But don't worry, darling, when you are buried deep inside me tonight, everything will be completely clear, okay, Hun?"

"Yeah well, okay, absolutely. That's fine with me," responded Chris with a smile, completely blown away by this erotic beauty. "Now what would you like for dinner?" responded Chris with a smile, realizing that he was caught totally in her magical web. Her perfume had him totally immobilized. Chris was floating on a cloud, and she, whoever she was, couldn't have been more pleased. She had hit the jackpot!

"Listen, Darling, I think it would be really exciting for us to tell each other our names, but only after you have penetrated me. It will be so exciting to make love with a complete stranger, without even knowing each other's names. What do you think, Darling?" she said with a great big smile on her face after another passionate kiss.

Chris just smiled. "Look, you and your intoxicating perfume have completely blown me away, and with your gorgeous, unbelievable, and sensational looks, you have me completely in your control. I'll do whatever you want, my beautiful one."

"Wonderful! Thank you, Darling." She laughed. "You know, Darling, I think we are really going to have a wonderful and a very rewarding time together. I can feel it. We are going to be just great together! This is almost magical. I am still amazed that I have found you like this. You know fate told me to come here tonight and told me where to find you, and yes, you were there, so I knew right away that we would be passionate lovers, and for the time that you are here, we would be together."

As it turned out, she was a freshman at the nearby college studying psychology, and she was someone special, that was for sure. Her father was, in fact, a very wealthy Russian businessman whom he obviously hadn't met.

The beautiful young lady and Chris both enjoyed a roast chicken dinner and a salad and some apple pie smothered with whipped cream.

After the delicious dinner, they had a few more drinks, and then they danced a little to the slow tunes that the band was playing. When they danced, she was stuck to him like glue, and she could feel his arousal and was pleased. Simultaneously he could even feel her sensuous body tight against his. He could even feel her heart beating against his chest. It was incredible.

"I think it is time we need to go to My Condo and get to know each other a little more intimately, Darling, don't you think?" she suggested with her sensuous, inviting smile.

"Absolutely," responded Chris enthusiastically.

Outside the restaurant/bar, they climbed into her Red Corvette. Before she had started the car, her soft hand had found his zipper. Immediately she had him in her mouth. "Mmm, Baby, this is just a prelude to what will happen tonight once we get to My Condo!" she said softly, licking her lips and laughing sensuously. Chris was already floating on a cloud somewhere. "But now, regretfully, I have to drive," she said with a smile.

With her driving her red rocket as if she was driving in some Le Mans race somewhere, they flew back into the city, and within minutes, they were parked in the basement garage of her condo tower, passionately making out as she stroked him so delicately, so softly with her long fingers wrapped around him firmly.

"Let's go up to our soft comfortable bed so I can show you delights you have never seen or felt before, Darling," she said with a smile. She was already hot!

*   *   *

As soon as the Oriental dream girl and Chris were through the door, and as soon as the door was locked behind them, she immediately wrapped her arms around Chris again and pulled him to her. They kissed each other passionately, open mouthed, and dueled with their tongues.

Slowly they came apart, still wrapped in each other's arms. "Oh, Chris, that was so wonderful. You cannot imagine. You know, Darling, tonight we will explore the universe all night long. Don't you fall asleep on me," she said cheekily, so overjoyed by the moment. Who really was this mystery man that she had just met and was about to make love with all night long? It was incredible. How things had changed!

Then in the background as she was pouring out two glasses of cold Chardonnay, the CD player clicked in, and Diana Krall gave them both some more encouragement.

> Let's fall in love,
> Why shouldn't we fall in love?
> Our hearts are made for it
> Let's take a chance,
> Why be afraid of it

Once inside her condo, she hung up her jacket in the closet, and then she sensuously suggested that Chris slip off her shoes from her dainty feet, which Chris willingly did, kissing and licking her bare feet as she smiled. Yes, she now knew she had hit the jackpot. This guy was special.

Then with a glass of wine in each other's hands, they slowly, arm in arm, moved out to the secluded balcony. After another sip of wine, it was back to the passionate kissing again. As they settled onto the comfortable soft couch, they cuddled and kissed some more.

Suddenly she jumped up and slipped out of her amazing silky wraparound dress, exposing herself in her purple lingerie to Chris, who was certainly now completely aroused by her sensuous and voluptuous body.

"You like?" she asked mischievously.

"Oh God, without question I like!" Chris smiled. He was being seduced by this gorgeous Oriental exotic beauty, and he loved it.

She was thrilled. After another sip of wine, she lifted her legs onto his lap. She could already feel his arousal. "Hey, mister, massage my legs a little si vous plait," she said in her sexy voice.

Chris softly caressed the sensitive skin of her inner thighs and slowly worked his way down her legs. She just loved the gentleness of his caresses. Everything with him was tender loving care, no rough treatment at all.

Now dressed only in her sexy lacy purple bra and her matching purple thong, she took his hand

and pulled him to his feet. Then without any hesitation, she removed his shirt, undid his belt, and pulled his slacks off him, along with his socks. Then she sensuously removed his shorts, exposing his already erect, well-endowed "friendly weapon," much to her pleasure. Without hesitation, she anxiously and almost hungrily performed fellatio on Chris.

With a sensuous smile, she took his hand and led him into the bedroom.

"No clothes allowed in this room," she said with a smile as she took off her bra and her thong. Chris was so overwhelmed by her sexual beauty and her unbelievable voluptuous now naked body. She had him totally in her control, and she loved it.

It had been a long time since she had been so sexually aroused. Her whole body shook with anticipation.

Then suddenly the two naked bodies were together, both totally aroused, kissing each other almost ravenously.

Let's close our eyes and make our own paradise
Little we know of it, still we can try
To make a go of it

"Listen, My Beautiful One, first I have to explore your gorgeous body all over and do some tender loving care treatment to you."

"I understand, my Darling, I know, my love, so you do whatever you like. I am yours tonight, and you are going to love me every which way all through the night. We have no inhibitions. I am loving every minute of this our first night of passionate love, the first night of many to come.''

> We might have an end for each other
> To be or not to be
> Let our Hearts discover

''Hey, Darling, I still don't know your name, but then again, God, you are so beautiful. Let me love you. Let me show you just I much a really care, right from the moment you walked into my life,'' he said softly. So, he positioned his angel and gently lay her on her back and began his explorations.

> Let's fall in love,
> Why shouldn't we fall in love
> Now is the time for it, while we can

He started at her head, kissing her beautiful face, her lips again, her closed eyes. He licked her ears and kissed and licked her throat. Slowly he reached her succulent breasts and strawberry-red nipples. He actually almost devoured her sensuous breasts and nipples as he spent a long, long time kissing, licking, and suckling on them, bringing her small orgasms she just couldn't believe. This was all new to her. He kissed and licked his way lower as his new young erotic lover softly moaned at the pleasure and sensations she was feeling.

She sighed loudly, but he just kissed and licked it sensuously.

Then he jumped on the floor and gave all his attention to her delicate, sensitive feet and long shapely legs, kissing and licking her toes and feet, bringing smiles to her again. God, this was so wonderful. Chris was really giving her a long sexual experience that she had never experienced before. No, she was no virgin, but her past lovers were amateurs compared to Chris. God, she was so loving this. Fate was really looking after her now.

Finally, Chris climbed back on her bed, raised her legs over his shoulders as he moved back between her legs, and slowly he began to orally stimulate her; he opened her up and used his tongue to penetrate her, which was sending her into another dimension. She now moaned loudly as she reached three powerful orgasms all in a row as Chris continued to stimulate her.

Finally, Chris moved up and looked at her. "Are you ready, Darling?"

Let's fall in love

"Oh yes, Darling, I have been waiting for this all night. Penetrate me now, in all my locations, my Darling! Now, my Darling! Make love to me, my Darling. God, this is so great," she responded softly.

Let's fall in love

And so, the night of ravenous sex and passionate love began as Chris penetrated her fully and powerfully. He began to make passionate love to his beautiful Oriental angel in every conceivable position possible to two passionate lovers. She was really amazed at the prowess of Chris and how sex could be so good, so fantastic, and so wonderful. She hoped it would never end. They did everything, positions that she never even knew existed and new ones they created themselves. She really was totally beside herself and so wonderfully overwhelmed by feelings she had never experience until now.

Let's fall in love

Finally, as the sun began to bring light back to the world, they both collapsed from exhaustion. "God, my Darling, which galaxy did you take me to? I want to go back there every night. That was the best sex I have ever had, ever. It was absolutely amazing.

"Don't you ever leave me. You know, I am going to want you now every night that you are available. Oh, my Darling, oh my Darling," she sighed in a whisper as she drifted off to sleep.

Then Chris too fell asleep wrapped around her.

Let's fall in love

It certainly was a night neither would ever forget. Fortunately, last night was a Friday night, so they had all day Saturday free to catch up on some sleep.

*   *   *

"Okay, Darling, finally," she said with a smile.

Both were still naked, with Chris lying on top of her, buried deep inside her, her full breasts and nipples pressing hard against his chest.

"For your information, my name is Kimiko Katherine Zemanova. My mother, Kyoto, was Japanese, and my father, Ivan, was Russian," she said with her cute smile. "They met in Paris, in France, and it was there in a small historical church that they got married, and it was there that I was born a few years ago." She let out a sensuous laugh.

"Now that you know all about me, tell me all about you, my love. I'm dying to know. It is so amazing that Fate has brought us together like this."

"Well, my name is now Chris Canyon. At one stage, I was Eric Baldwin, until my Uncle Dwayne Baldwin, the godfather of the South, killed my Mother and Father—his brother—with a car bomb. I managed to miraculously to survive. That was back in Lexington., Kentucky."

"With both my parents dead, he also tried to kill me again, but that attempt didn't material-ize either! After he beat the crap out of me, he left me in a ditch by the roadside assuming I was dead, but I got some help from Fate and from another unknown family, and I survived. So at that point, with the advice from the Doctor and the FBI, I changed my name. Now when I become a Navy SEAL, I'll be able to go back to Kentucky to get my revenge and take care of business and my sadistic Uncle."

"Oh, my god, how sad! Well, Darling, you need not worry, as I will train you, along with the SEALs, into a perfect male specimen. The SEALs will train you in all the various skills that you will need, mentally, physically, in endurance, toughness, espionage knowledge, weapons, and so on.

"I will, however, train you in passion, mental skills, and the delicate techniques of lovemaking. Yes, Darling, I deal with the soft, gentle side of life! We will enjoy all our passionate training sessions together. We will endure long and intense passionate sessions to make sure you will be able to withstand these long grueling train sessions, and believe me, I will really look after you. Your body will be so alive, you won't believe it, but you will love every minute of it." She laughed softly.

Yes, their training sessions were long and hard, and both were totally exhausted, but with great big smiles on their faces. Both were totally satisfied.

For the remaining time he spent at the academy, before they started sending him around the world, Kimiko really did look after him. Sexually Chris had never been so fulfilled before. She was an expert when it came to sexual passion. She was the best! In a very short time, Chris knew the delicacy of her body and where all her sensitive points were, so he could totally satisfy her, just like she was able to satisfy him.

But the fact was that Chris could not get Kiara out of his mind, and the sex he had with Kimiko and the other girls just was great but not the same. It just didn't compare, which really didn't surprise him, not that there was anything wrong with these young ladies, far from it, especially Kimiko. Yes, that passion and the lust and sexual excitement was there, but they just weren't Kiara!

Simply, he loved Kiara. She was the love of his life.

After completing his training all around the world at different US bases, he was finally shipped to Broome in Western Australia, to the US base there.

In Broome, in Western Australia, the beautiful bronzed blonde Aussie shielas already knew the score. They had experienced these SEALs before. They were there to entertain the SEALs and the other US servicemen. They knew there was no future or long-term relationships pending, so they just enjoyed themselves whenever they got together, and yes, the sex was enjoyable but again only temporary.

Kiara Tasha Taylor

For Kiara, her three years, was quite different. It was something she had never expected and it certainly was an eye-opening experience, to say the least! She was not prepared to experience the world of college life, or should we rephrase that to "the world of college sex life."

Yes, for Kiara, it was somewhat different as she teamed up with her roommates, who just happened to be a couple of gorgeous, full-bodied, vivacious, sensuous young brunettes—April Anderson and Bambie Beaumont—who were at college for partying, lots of fun, and lots and lots of sex with a variety of males, and yes, some females too. Kiara was instantly caught in that web.

Thus all three girls were all certainly desirable from a male's point if view—full 38" busts, full hips, beautiful faces with luscious full lips, and their perfect derrieres for other erotic activities, and most importantly, they all loved passionate sex in all its forms. Education really was secondary to most of these young ladies, but Kiara was still was intent on getting her degrees for her future as a doctor.

Weekends became reserved for frat and associated parties. Wednesday nights were the girls' night out by themselves and the subsequent lesbian activities back in their dorm room, after the dinner as they hungrily explored each other's delicious bodies, head to toe, and at times they usually invited other young ladies to join them, usually one or three to make up the couples.

So Kiara got to taste the both sides of the spectrum, sex with males and females.

The three girls hooked up with various guys for party activities the college way.

First, there was the large group gatherings, and there was always some wild exhibitionist-type females who were quite prepared to provide oral sex to numerous miscellaneous guys while everyone watched and applauded and screamed encourage- ment. Some even had sex with various guys while others again watched. It was all exciting and fun— the college way!

Kiara would have nothing to do with these kind of group activities.

And the three girls were all in agreement that if drugs ever showed up at any of their parties or get-togethers, they were out of there. None of them wanted anything to do with drugs and spe- cifically the physical, emotional, and then the legal consequences.

Next the girls also agreed to certain ground rules:

1. There had to be total respect for the girls.
2. No physical force or any violence whatsoever.
3. No submissive bullshit.
4. No photographs, period! All phones and cameras were put away for the duration of the parties.

If any one of the three guys broke the rules, all three girls were gone.

Initially it was just a little fun at these private parties with the three guys and the three girls. It started out with some dancing and then some drinking and casual conversations, which quickly developed into passionate make-out sessions with the three guys, who were by now all groping the luscious females and their sexy bodies.

Yes, in the heat of those moments, Kiara too joined in. Then the oral sex pursued, with the girls providing the oral stimulation and entertainment to the three guys, switching partners regularly at that stage. Soon the clothes came off, and obviously, the next thing was the girls having passionate sex with the three guys. Then through the night, they switched partners again quite regularly so that the girls got to experience the attributes and talents of each of the three guys. So by morning, all three girls would have had passionate sex with all three guys numerous times.

Yes, it was also true that all three girls had had sex with their applicable boyfriends back home, but this was totally different! Now on each weekend, they teamed up with three different guys and were each enjoying sex with the three different guys each time at multiple times through the nights.

Usually during the course of the night, there also would have been the DPs or double penetrations and, of course, the anal penetrations.

For Kiara, these were the highlights, the most erotic parts of the nights. Kiara just loved the anal penetrations as they were quite different to the regular sex, and the intensity of the anal sex really excited her. She loved it.

Satisfying two guys at once, allowing two males to penetrate her at the same time was also really wild and exciting for each of these three girls, as they were now experiencing all the different variations and activities for the first time. They were really enjoying it, as they all put out enthusiastically, especially now, when they were totally uninterrupted, being away from home.

Kiara got caught in the rotating sexual environment and action, and at these types of parties, unequivocal sex was always on the menu.

Kiara acknowledged, the sexual lust was certainly enjoyable, especially the double penetrations and the anal penetrations, which she loved. Kiara certainly enjoyed having her naked body ravished, penetrated, explored, and caressed by three different sets of hands each weekend. It was great. There was something erotic about sex with complete strangers. It was all new, different, and certainly exciting.

Did Kiara care for any of these guys? Hell no! It was sex for the sake of sex. Feelings? None existed! It was just out-and-out sex and sexual release and new and different sensations! Did the guys care for any of the girls? Of course not. No, not at all. It was just lust!

For the girls, love never entered the picture. That was only a word, and one that was not used at any of these parties. It was all physical lust and passionate sex, and who the partners were really was irrelevant and didn't matter, as they changed weekly. The girls with the full bodies were always in demand for these intimate get-togethers, so Kiara was always in demand.

Kiara, being as beautiful as she was and having a full vivacious body had numerous requests by various guys to get into some form of relationship, but she obviously had no interest in those, as she was officially already in a relationship with Chris. But yes, she was in demand, and consequently, she was able to select those guys that did appeal to her.

Kiara did nothing in a crowd, but at private parties, things were totally different. And it was peer pressure initially, but Kiara didn't argue the point—she just joined in. If her two roommates indulged in passionate sex with the guys, then it was expected that she too should join in as well, and she did it quite voluntarily and willingly! The fact was, she loved uninhibited sex in all its forms.

Their boyfriends back home? Who were they?

So she was introduced to college sex. Typically the three girls usually were involved with three guys, never the same three; all were different. So Kiara ended up having sex with a large number of guys she had never seen before, and as it was all physical, she really enjoyed these weekend sex-capades. Yes, there were no feelings involved, only lust and the thrill of another naked body penetrating her, with the physical enjoyment of sex.

Love was never in the picture, and love never entered any of the circumstances.

Then suddenly the first year came to an abrupt end. She had managed to pass all her courses with relatively good grades, for which she was happy. In some ways, the sexual encounters removed any mental sexual frustration and stress that she would have had if she hadn't participated in the party scene with her two voluptuous roommates.

As she headed back home to reality, for the summer season, she could not believe just what she had done that first year. Initially she felt guilty and thought that she had actually cheated on Chris, but thinking it through, she acknowledged that she wasn't cheating. Chris knew that they would both indulge in sex with others, and even though she had really enjoyed her sexual encounters with all the various guys, she realized more and more just how much Chris really meant to her.

Of all the guys that she had had sex with, not one of them came even close to what Chris did to her. The fact that she loved Chris and Chris loved her was obviously the major factor in their sexual activities. That was why she had fallen so in love with him in the first place. But now with all the various partners she had had and all the various sexual activities she had indulged in, she realized just how good sex with Chris really had been.

In her own mind, she had come to terms with what she had done. Now with the experience with all the different guys, she knew she now would be a more experienced and more of an active partic-ipant with Chris when he returned.

Yes, it was sex with a variety of other guys, but it was totally meaningless. The only part that she enjoyed was the actual physical sexual sensa-tions she experienced during the act, but then it was all over, and, yes, totally meaningless. Did she remember any of the guys she had sex with? No!

For her next two years, she switched universi-ties and attended Oklahoma University. There no one knew her, and now she was in total control of her own life and her activities at the college level. This time her studies came first, and her grades improved dramatically.

She attended numerous parties, but only joined in on some selected ones. Yes, she still had meaningless sex with some of the guys, but only once in a while. But then she did arrange to get together with two guys at the same time for the double penetrations that she loved, but she was not looking for any relationships.

She knew these were only temporary. When Chris returned, he would be there to take her to paradise again, and she now accepted that sex with love, specifically Chris's love, was far greater than anything she had experienced in college.

Chris was always there in the back of her mind. She now really looked forward to their next three-way trip to the constellations again with Alycia.

Part 2

The Change in the Political Arena

Chapter 18

The State of the Union

While Chris was immersed in the Navy SEAL training program and Kiara studied hard to become a doctor, the United States was leading up to another Presidential Election, another farce and another example of complete corruption by the Political Fat Cats, the One Percent Super Rich, and the corrupt, greedy Corporations.

The last eight years had been a disaster. With the first African American president, everyone hoped and prayed that now a change would come about for the average Americans, who had been suffering severely with out-of-date bureaucracy in both federal and state politics and financially under the incompetent and money-hungry Bush-and-Cheney Combination. Unfortunately, and alas, this new President was restricted from doing anything. His own Party was too scared to rock the boat. When he had the majority, he didn't use it and when he lost the majority, he couldn't do anything. The Two-Party System, as usual, brought everything to a halt!

So nothing ever got done; nothing was ever accomplished.

It became obvious that He too was there only for the money and political connections, so he too could join the elite American 1% Rich Club.

So the next eight years had been much the same, the same old in-house fighting between the two Parties, the headstrong Republicans and the cautious (don't-rock-the-boat) Democrats; consequently, nothing happened, nothing was accomplished. Compromise? Are you kidding? Both parties believed in the "My Way or the Highway" principle, so yes, nothing was accomplished!

The fact that the American infrastructure was falling apart—the highways, the overpasses, the bridges, everything needed to be refurbished, repaired, or replaced—was acknowledged by everyone. Did any politician care? Of course not! They couldn't have cared less. They were doing fine. They were Compensation Packages were simply out of this World.

It was a fact that anyone becoming a new Senator or a House Representative, they automatically received benefits that they all had voted in for themselves behind closed doors.

So what did they care about the average American, the tax payers, the destroyed middle class, the poor, the homeless, the mentally ill, the ill, and the veterans? Nothing! Yes, absolutely nothing!

The combination of Bush and Cheney certainly didn't care. They had taken care of their rich and wealthy friends through their two questionable terms, in the process destroying the middle class in the infamous "Bush Crash," as the Middle Class lost fortunes that they had worked hard and long to accumulate. Gone, yes, gone, like a puff of smoke! Gone!

No one ever explained why or how! No one was ever blamed! The Middle Class had just disappeared, and George and Dick just sat there with their wealthy friends, stupid smiles on their faces, counting their millions! How many millions of dollars had been wasted? How many soldiers' lives had been lost? And for what?

Yes, George W. Bush would go down in history as one of the worst Presidents on Record.

But Hey, Bush and Cheney were paid for life. How wonderful! Even after all the corruption they had generated, even after all that the Rich had taken from the Middle Class, they still received paychecks for the rest of their lives. Why?

What did they do to help the average American? Absolutely nothing!

They spent millions, billions of dollars to fight an illegal war based on lies and distorted facts, so they could get their hands on Iraq's "oil." What about the thousands of soldiers that lost their lives, American and allies, what about them? Their families? The Iraqi people themselves?

"We thought that Saddam had Weapons of Mass Destruction."

"Thought?" Yeah, right! What a bunch of crap!

George W. Bush, in his stupidity, declared that they were selling Democracy to the Middle East, and Iraq would be the first model Democratic State in the Middle East region. How could he sell Democracy to the Middle East when Democracy in the United States had left long ago! It didn't exist in the United States, and it hadn't now for quite some time. So how could He be selling, something that didn't exist?

Yes, the clueless President of America, President George W. Bush, had no idea what Democracy even meant!

What existed now was a Government by the Rich, for the Rich, and that included all the Federal and State Politicians, and we could not forget the Supreme Court, or was it really "the Supreme Circus"? Yes, all paid for by the Rich!

At that point, the legitimacy of both the George Bushes' Terms, decided by the bought and misguided Supreme Court, still remains questionable! The legitimate course of history had been manipulated by Corruption right at the highest levels!

Chapter 19

The New Federal Elections

The fact was that the so-called United States was in a mess. The Popularity of the Federal Government, which included the President, the senate, the House of Representatives, and indirectly the Supreme Court, which everyone knew had been bought by the super rich, was at a staggering low of 7 percent. Yes, 7 percent, which basically confirmed that the Federal Government was doing absolutely nothing for the country!

Did President Bush or VP Cheney care? Did the politicians really care?

Of course, not! Why should they? For them everything was just fine!

But my God, the Politicians were certainly lining their own pockets with everything they could get their hands on. Whether they were Republicans or Democrats, it didn't matter. Their only interest was in making more money for themselves. The

Affairs of the Country and the welfare of the common people were totally irrelevant.

How many US and Allied soldiers died in these supposed legal wars was again irrelevant.

Did these wars ever achieve anything? No! Just look at Iraq and Afghanistan now, after the billions of dollars the United States spent/wasted…And all the lives lost!

Yes, the Country was in a turmoil. The only thing that was happening was that the Rich got richer and the increasing poor got poorer. George W Bush and his partner in crime, Cheney, had destroyed the Middle Class! The Bush Crash had devastated millions, but not the Rich; the poor lost fortunes, the Rich got richer, and no one to this day ever got blamed, no one!

The sad part was that the average American had no idea how much these Politicians were taking home in cash and benefits, and without even working for it! With a 7 percent popularity, they obvious were not working! Not working!

What about the people that voted them in? What about them?

Who were they?

Frankly, they, the average people, really didn't even count—not in the least!

Democracy had failed miserably, and there was President Bush trying to sell Democracy to the Middle East when he didn't even have it in the so-called United States! What a joke!

The United States? Come on and face reality, there never has been the United States.

Each State, each Governor, did and does exactly what they wanted. They made laws that suited them, milked the Federal Government for whatever they could, and ignored Federal Laws when they chose to, and all dictated by the local leeches or parasites, the Governor and his Cronies, who, like all of the existing American Politicians, cared nothing for the citizens of his State, but only for himself and his fellow Politicians, the other blood suckers, the 1 percenters who where only there to make as much money as they could for themselves!

Yes, President, George W. Bush, even after technically losing both elections, the money and the corrupt-bought Supreme Court, also known as the "Supreme Circus" bought him the Presidency, much to the disappointment of the American people.

So George and Dick set about to invade Iraq with lies, supposedly to help bring Democracy to Iraq. Did Iraq want Democracy? Hell No! But George and Dick wanted the oil—more money!

So George invaded Iraq for the oil. Thousands of American and Allied soldiers were killed unnecessarily, not to mention all the innocent Iraqi people themselves. But George and Dick didn't care. After destroying Iraq, George set about destroying America with his famous "George W. Bush Crash," which destroyed the American Middle Class completely. Millions lost their life savings, yet no one was ever blamed for that disaster. But Hey, the Rich certainly got richer! George and Dick kept on smiling!

Yes, the Federal Government was a joke!

Then finally an African American became president, and everyone rejoiced, but not for long. He too had fooled the public. The fact was, his own Party restricted him from doing anything, so again, for the next eight years, nothing of any consequence happened, but upon his termination, he too became part of the 1% rich. Meanwhile the general public was being raped by their own Government. Income taxes on the rich were relaxed. Yes, the rich got richer, and the poor became an increasing number. The senseless battle between the Republicans and the Democrats continued.

So, with a new election coming up, the voters had to look at their options. The problem was, there were no options. The Republicans vs. the Democrats…yes, there was no option. One was as bad as the other.

The Republicans and the Democrats, in essence, were the same. All the Politicians were money-hungry stock and now part of the 1% rich.

Then suddenly, totally out of the blue, and totally unexpectedly, there appeared a glimmer of hope.

Suddenly a disillusioned Democrat, a senior Senator, Samuel Bateman, had decided to quit the Democratic Party and to run as an Independent and with a far different and radical platform from the Democrats and Republicans.

Both the Republican and Democratic leaders just laughed. "Don't worry, as an Independent, who will listen to him? Financially he won't get anywhere! Relax, he's totally a loser, a hoax. He has no support. We'll bury him. He's just like that other loser, Ross Perrault, from years ago!"

Ross Perrault's intensions were the same as Samuel's, except that Ross presented the overall financial picture, which the average folks did not understand, but Samuel presented just what the politicians were stealing from the General Public, specifically only for themselves, and that the Average American understood!

So the Democrats ignored Samuel Bateman completely as he had already quit their party anyway, and they had already nominated the glamourous, beautiful Louise Elizabeth Cambridge, a wealthy New Yorker socialite and State Politician, who was already part of the 1% rich club, as their Presidential Candidate.

The Republicans had Reginald Wallace Garfield, the wonder Boy, the All-American ex-college football star, as their nominated candidate. The only problem with Reginald was that, he had very little Political experience, but he looked like a young John Kennedy and a young Robert Redford (from the movie *The Candidate*), the desired image to lead the youth of the country to victory.

Reginald also lacked brains, but again the Republican Leaders knew he could be manipulated and placed a sharp young ambitious lawyer, Lance Albright, as his spokesperson.

The Leaders of the Democrats and the Republicans had no fear of Samuel Bateman, the old-timer who had had his day and was now no threat to them. In fact, they were so confident that Samuel had no chance in hell against two established powerhouse parties, the Democrats and the Republicans! They never even bothered to read his platform initially.

Yes, they had not seen his platform of reform that he was proposing to sell to the General Public, the People of the United States. The Super Rich would bury him, but the Super Rich were only a Minority Group. Yes, they were rich, but the General Public had the votes!

And Votes in this Election were important!

Little did they realize that Samuel Bateman's platform could destroy their Political Gravy Train!

Chapter 20

The Political Candidates

Yes...The **New Presidential Race** was on.

Ironically the Republicans and the Democrats lived in a separate World, the World of the One Percent Rich. They completely ignored the inevitable public opinion; the Presidential race would be won by either a Republican or a Democrat, as it had been for generations.

The Democrats

The Democratic Leaders were so confident that Samuel Bateman, whatever he did or proposed, would just be buried in the wash. He was no longer a Democrat and who were these so-called Independents? Just pesky flies!

The Democrats obviously ignored their Rebel Senator from New Hampshire, Samuel Bateman, and his revolutionary Platform that could destroy the politicians "Gravy Train "Life Style. His ideas were revolutionary and radical, and they wanted no part of him or his ideas. Besides, he was only one single individual to individually take on the two Political Powerhouses, the Republicans and the Democrats—the residents of La, La, Land!

So they nominated a popular celebrity, Louise Cambridge from New York, who was already in the one percent super rich classifications, but with little or no federal government experience. She was the Governor of New York, yes, she was a woman, but she was also a Fat Cat. Irrespective, the Democrat Leaders were confident that she would sway the American women voters in the United States to their Party.

The Republicans

Yes, they had their new wonder boy—a young handsome ex-college football star, Reginald Wallace Garfield, who was totally clueless on politics, but he represented the new JFK. Yes, the new Kennedy image candidate, but digging deeper, he was the epitome of the character portrayed so brilliantly by Robert Redford in the movie The Candidate, who, once he had won his nomination, said, "What do I do now?"

The Republican caucus was confident that the young candidate would sway the younger generation back to them. But, they would pursue the standard Republican platform across the board. The Republican Leaders were confident that they had the best chance of winning. After all, the white American macho males couldn't see a woman as a President!

The Independents

At the start of the Election, there was only one Independent candidate, and that was Samuel Bateman. However, Samuel was not another Ross Perrault. He knew that to win, he needed Independent Candidates in each of the States; individually he could do nothing, so his plan was to wake up the American Populace and hopefully attract enough caring Candidates to join his Party.

For the first time in American History, unexpectedly a new Party emerged from the downtrodden American populace—the new Independent Party, led by the renegade Democratic Senator, the senior Samuel Bateman, who had been a Democrat for years, from New Hampshire, one of the Conservative New England States. He had decided he needed change for the sake of the country that he had loved, which had been forsaken by the Super Rich, their puppets, and the Federal and State Politicians.

The Democrats all laughed at him and just ignored him, but Samuel was a true American, and he still believed in "By the People and For the People." In the modern-day politics, the greed and corruption had set in, and the Federal Government was a joke. The Politicians were there only for the money and absolutely nothing else, just more and more money for themselves.

Samuel knew he had only one shot at this, as he was not a millionaire or billionaire, but he had his daughter, Julia Elizabeth Bateman, for physical and mental support, but his best friend was a billionaire, Robert Alexander Hampton, who provided him with support and encouragement as well.

In his travels around the Country, he found unofficially quite a lot of support sitting in the sidelines. In fact, there were many people, whom he spoke to, who supported his ideals.

So Samuel Bateman took the bull by the horns, knowing he had a huge mountain to climb, way bigger than Everest, but he knew he had to try.

At that point in time, the popularity of the Federal Government was at an embarrassing seven percent, which basically proved that this Government, the Congress, the Senate, the House of Representatives, and one might as well include the Supreme Court, or better known as the Supreme Circus, was not functioning at all. But did the Politicians care? Of course, not! Why should they? Everything was rosy for them. Lots of money, no work, Yes, basically it was still the party mode!

The fact was the two-party system of Government just wasn't functioning at all, the continual bickering, the cat fights, the filibusters, anything to avoid making a decision. In fact, they had already brought the government to a standstill, and sadly the Politicians were proud of it. How it affected the common people, they didn't care.

Compromise, are you kidding? They didn't even know the word existed!

Help the people of the country? What for? They were having a ball!

Look after their constituents?

Who the hell were they?

Over the years, unbeknownst to the American public, these phonies, these Fat Cats, had voted themselves unbelievable benefits, benefits that no one else in the country had, not even the corporate CEOs.

So what made these money-hungry Politicians think that they were so special to deserve these benefits when in fact they did nothing to help the average and underprivileged Americans and the country itself?

Their own greed!

The fact was once an individual became a Senator or a House Representative, with their new benefits, they automatically became part of the country's one percent Super Rich.

Their Job Descriptions basically were ……. do nothing, entertain your friends at expensive steak houses, and let the taxpayers foot the bills, then get paid for the rest of your life, even if you did absolutely nothing! Great salary, free medical, unavailable to the other Americans, free travel, etc.

It was no wonder everyone wanted to be a Politician. It was the easiest free ride on the planet! No work, just play, and only if you wanted to, then take the check home and live the life of Riley in your mansion wherever, preferably away from the riff-raff.

By serving only one term, the Politician now was entitled to full salary for the rest of his life. Welcome to the one percent of the Super Rich Club.

Chapter 21

The Independent Movement

Samuel Bateman, over the years, had watched the greed of the Politicians and the corruption of the Super Rich and the Corporations increase steadily while the welfare of the country and its everyday, common people were just ignored completely. Consequently, they all were having a difficult time coping!

Samuel Bateman was totally disillusioned with the present protocol: the Country and its Citizens were totally ignored, and neither Party was about to make amends to correct the situation. They were too busy looking after themselves. Meanwhile, Samuel had been making notes as to all the issues that needed to be amended to make things right again.

Where are We going?

- The Federal Government is a joke.

- The Politicians' only interest is themselves; the welfare of the Citizens is irrelevant.
- The Supreme Court under George Bush has become a laughing stock when it declared that Corporations were, in fact, people.
- The Two-Party system is always deadlocked to the various affairs of the Government, as the Republicans have vowed to make the first African American President to hold office totally incompetent. Their mandate was now to discredit the President to the "Nth" degree.
- So it was time to turn the tide on the corruption that was now rampant in the USA.
- Fifty states - all separate
- 1,100 counties - all independent
- Federal government — Non-functional
- Legal system and courts - A failure
- Federal compensation to States for inmates - A racket only for the benefit of the local Governors to add to their slush Funds
- Innocent people arrested for what? Irrelevant!

Samuel knew he had only one chance to achieve his platform, and that was to create another Party — the Independent Party, with Representatives in all the States, running against the Republicans and the Democrats. But he knew he had to educate the common people and make them understand the existing corruption, condition, and reality.

So Samuel bought a two-hour window on the main television networks on a Wednesday night to present his case and the formation of the new Independent Party and its revolutionary platform, to the attention of the American Public.

Samuel had brains, so after he had documented his platform, his manifesto, into simple terms, he purposely had leaked his carefully edited Manuscript of his radical platform to *New York Times*, *USA Today*, *Time Magazine*, and numerous other media organizations, taking in all the major cities in America a week before his television speech. His platform was suddenly in the hands of the other major United States Papers across the country, and suddenly there was an awakening in the populace. Thus, even before he had even stepped in front of the TV cameras, the papers had already alerted the Populace of his Platform.

The real fact was that the General Public was so fed up with the continual bickering between the two parties in Congress, with nothing ever being accomplished or done. The only ones that were doing well were the One Percent Super Rich and, of course, the Politicians themselves!

Samuel's Manuscript intended to change all that!

So that Wednesday night, Samuel proposed to change America forever.

Contrary to the belief of the Democratic and Republican Leaders, Samuel had lots of support, much more than he ever thought he had, much more than anyone had imagined, especially after his leaked platform having now spread across the country.

This was not another single-handed Ross Perrault campaign. This was becoming a full-fledged Independent Party campaign, with representatives in all the states.

Now for the first time, the American Populace was being told the truth about the Super Rich and the corrupt Politicians in Washington, much to their horror.

His headquarters was being run off its feet as they were signing up new members to the Independent Party. Anxious and concerned local individuals were calling his office to get information on how to organize an Independent base in their own states. It was like a tsunami; soon all States were now being represented by the Independent Party.

Samuel's daughter could not believe the impact that the leaked platform had had. It obviously had hit home right all across the Country.

Everyone in the various media outlets wanted an exclusive interview with Samuel. Local papers were all carrying the message across America. It was time to rock the boat, and the targets were the existing money-hungry Politicians and the One Percent Super Rich, both in Federal and State Politics.

Even all the State Politicians were scared. If the Independents came into power, their State gravy trains would also quickly end.

Chapter 22

The Awakening

After five days of absolute panic, the nation's newspapers were running out of copies of their reprints. They were all sold out as the Populace had bought out all the copies of Samuel Bateman's proposed platform to bring in a new America, an America that had existed and that George W. Bush and his buddy Cheney had driven in the final nails, subsequently destroyed the middle class and rewarded the Rich big time.

Julia and Robert, in Samuel's headquarters in New Hampshire, were shocked and absolutely elated at the sudden extensive interest that had swept the Nation. Everyone was talking about Samuel Bateman and his Bateman Manifesto.

Also, they were shocked when international messages came in from around the world, rejoicing and praising the Bateman Manuscript. Reality would return to America.

The shock also hit the Leaders of Democrats and the Republicans. Now as they read the Manifesto, they all just about had heart attacks. How could this lone individual create such an uproar? Suddenly all the volunteers for the Democrats and the Republicans made their way to the newly opened offices of the Independent Party in all the various states.

Everyone was now waiting for Samuel's television broadcast.

Finally, the Country had woken up, and suddenly there was real interest in the platforms that each of the parties had documented, but only the Independents were telling the truth. All that the Republicans and the Democrats could do was blame each other for the continual deadlocks, the filibusters, the bickering, and the inability to accomplish anything. Frankly they were not interested in anything, only if there were some benefits coming their way. The Country, the Average People, the Populace, who cared? Certainly, not the Politicians.

Even the town hall meetings became centers of interest. As the Independents caught the attention of the Public. The assigned attempts by the Democrats and the Republican to disrupt these meetings were quickly squashed by special army, navy, and air force soldiers assigned by the forces to maintain law and order. The local police forces were pushed aside by orders from the FBI and by the military forces, who were now all supporting Daniel Bateman and the Independents.

Quickly the Republicans and the Democrats tried desperately to abandon these town hall meeting, but without success. The local Democratic and Republican Representatives refused to attend, fearing for their own safety.

Thus, the support for the Independents grew daily.

Chapter 23

Samuel Bateman's Platform

Finally, Samuel Jeremiah Bateman fronted up, under heavy FBI guard, and totally unannounced to the local media, at the TV studio with his daughter, Julia, and his best and lifelong friend Robert, an actual billionaire with their own bodyguards as well, to broadcast his much-anticipated and awaited declaration of the Independent's Party election campaign Platform.

By this time, all the Country knew about it, and all wanted to see and hear the calm calculating Samuel emphasize just how much the American Populace had suffered under the past administrations with the two various Presidents.

- The FBI was determined to make sure nothing happened to Samuel Bateman.
- The fact was that the heads of CIA and FBI were all supporting Samuel Bateman, as

they too were tired of the lies, the arrogance and nonsense of the existing pompous Politicians. Respect for each other had totally disappeared. Everything was based on the dollar! Every time a problem came out of Congress, the CIA and the FBI were always the scapegoats.

- The truth was always covered up, and innocent individuals blamed.
- Surprisingly even the Armed Services, the Army, the Navy, and the Air Force supported Samuel Bateman as well, and they sent out teams to support the FBI all for the protection of the Independent Candidates.
- Everyone, except the Politicians and the One Percent Rich and the numerous multimillion-dollar Corporations, agreed that it was vital that Samuel's message was broadcast to the American people. The people needed to wake up to the reality and reclaim their own country from the Fat Cats and the greedy Corporations.
- Consequently, the American People were glued to their TV sets, and those without TVs all hit the local bars to hear the message from Samuel Bateman, outlining his totally revolutionary platform to turn the country back to the people of America again and then to re-establish the Middle Class again.

This was what Samuel intended to do with a Majority Independent Government.

Finally, sitting in a comfortable Eames chair, Samuel Bateman began his two-hour policy declaration.

"Good evening, my dear friends and all true Americans. Tonight we have a very special message to the American people. This is definitely something everyone needs to understand!"

"Tonight, we will outline the basic amendments that we, the Independent Party, will introduce and apply to Federal and State Governments and Politics to bring this great Country of ours out of the hands of the One Percent Super Rich and our greedy Politicians, Federally and State wise, and the bought Supreme Court, back into the hands of the People of America, as our Forefathers intended it to be.

"Let's face it, the average American has been raped by the policies introduced by our greedy Federal and State Politicians for far too long. Politics is not a boys' club. It is supposed to represent the People of America, and I stress, *all* the people of America, not just the super One Percent Rich, as is the case now.

"Even our Supreme Court is a joke and full of bought judges that cater only to the two Parties, not the American people. I stress, *not* the American people! Changes will be made!

"First, let's discuss our Politicians—yes, me regretfully included, even though the official records will show that I, Samuel Bateman, voted against all these one-sided benefit packages. We will publish a long list of politicians who did vote these benefits in for themselves. Yes, that list is a long one.

"I am very sure that most Americans are not aware of what is happening in our Congress here in Washington, DC, today! The real fact is that **nothing** is happening here in Washington, DC. For the Politicians, it continues to be Party Mode, basically, because the only bills that get passed now are those that only benefit the One Percent Rich and the Politicians themselves, certainly not the average Americans! And these bills are never made public.

"Now, folks, pay attention. This is just the start of what our so-called elected Politicians earn every year, and I Stress...for life, that they have voted for themselves, along with benefits, which I will get to.

"The President earns $180,000 yearly while in office, and also for life, along with endless other benefits. House/Senate members earn $174,000 per year and for life, plus all the various benefits. The speaker of the house gets $223,500 per year and for life—yes, more than the President! Plus the benefits. And the Majority/Minority leaders get $223,500 per year and for life—again more than the President—plus the benefits.

"In comparison, the average salary of a teacher is $ 40,065, no benefits. And a deployed soldier, $38,000, no benefits.

"In additions to the Politicians' basic salaries, they have the best medical plan of anyone in America, or on this planet, and for them, it's free. They have holidays like no one else working in America has! And I stress the word **holidays.** Frankly, their time in Washington is already a holiday for them as they have not achieved anything or done anything for the average Americans.

"Free meals at the taxpayers' expense, free travel at the taxpayers' expense—frankly, who do these politicians really believe they are to deserve these kinds of benefits? Gods? These are benefits that they voted for themselves. Why do they have a special medical plan when the rest of the population of Americans *do not* have a national plan to speak of! Why? Because these politicians have no plans to introduce a national health plan for the rest of you folks.

"Next, why can the Politicians and the Super Rich hide their fortunes offshore? To avoid paying taxes on their money that they have accumulated in America.

"There are other issues that we will highlight this evening. Let's look at what the Independent Party will do if we can get a majority in both the House and the Senate.

The Independent's Manifesto

- Amend and revise the pay packages of the Presidents, Senators, House Representatives,

Supreme Court judges, in fact, all Politicians and bring them in line with the pay packages offered to the average American people. Eliminate all lifetime packages for Politicians, past and present.

"Let's face it, politicians are not God's, and they have proved that they are doing nothing, absolutely nothing, for the average people. We propose, for Senators /House Representatives, pay packages for work done: no work, no pay.

It should be an honor to be selected to a working committee, not an automatic pay raise. Basically no tenure/no pension."

- Congressmen/women collect a salary while in office and receive no pay when they're out of office."
- Congress (past, present, and future) participates in Social Security. All funds in the Congressional retirement fund is to be moved to the Social Security System immediately. All future funds flow into the Social Security System, and Congress participates with American people. It may not be used for any other purpose.
- Members of Congress can purchase their own retirement plan, just as all other Americans do!
- Congress will no longer vote themselves a pay raises. Congressional pay will rise by the lower of CPI or 3 percent. The level

of present compensation will be revised to a realistic level, not the sums presently handed out on a platter.

- Members of Congress lose their current health care system, which is presently available to them, and again for life, and then they can or will participate in the same health care system as all the American people. A suitable plan is yet to be determined. For sixteen years, they have talked about it, but the two parties cannot agree on anything, let alone a health plan. Perhaps if they didn't already have a plan for themselves, then they would be more prepared to discuss it?
- No free health care package for politicians. They, the Politicians, must buy with their own funds, from their own wages, packages that will also be available to the average American. Politicians are to pay for health care just like everyone else.
- Lobbyists for Corporations have become a virus and will be immediately and automatically outlawed, for everyone's interest. Lobbying (also persuasion) is the act of attempting to influence the actions, policies, or decisions of officials in their daily life, most often legislators or members of regulatory agencies. Professional lobbyists are people whose business is trying to influence legislation on behalf of a Group, a Corporation, or Individuals who has hired them.

The ethics and morality of lobbying are duel edged. Lobbying is often spoken of with contempt when the implication is that people with inordinate social economic power are corrupting the law (twisting it away from fairness) in order to serve their own interests. Basically when people who have a duty to act on behalf of others, such as elected officials with a duty to serve their constituents' interests or, more broadly, the public good, can benefit by shaping the law to serve the interests of some private parties, a conflict of interest, exists.

Henceforth, politicians cannot accept any kind or form of payments or gifts from any corporations. Any politician receiving or accepting compensation from any Corporation will be considered as accepting bribes and will be arrested. At times, these bribes could be in the millions. Nice?

- Corporations will need to understand that, henceforth, contracts will be awarded on Merit, and Merit alone, not because of the support of any particular Politician or Politicians, or any other influential group. Let's face it, folks, Corporations are **not** people. Amend specific laws accordingly.
- The Supreme Court is dismissed. New judges to be elected by the people, not bought by the Republicans, Democrats, or Corporations.

- Allow additional Parties into Government. Eliminate two-party politics as it does not work or function, as all the other civilized countries around the world have discovered long ago, and we have finally found out too! Period! Suggested new parties, in addition to the Democrats and the Republicans: Independent Party, Labour Party, Green Party, etc. Perhaps, one hopes that with three or more parties, the word **compromise** will again re-enter and be reintroduced into our language.
- Offshore money that the Wealthy and Politicians have been hiding in foreign accounts to avoid paying taxes in America will now stay offshore. Offshore funds will no longer be returned or transferred back to America. If they are brought back, it will be confiscated, and fines will be levied. Effective immediately.
- No compensation to the States for inmates. Inmates in each State are the State's own responsibility. Not a Federal responsibility, not something that the American people/taxpayer should have to pay for, specifically as the funds end up in the Governor's own slush fund. The inmates get no benefits from the federal handout! It will be hereby cancelled.

"Do you folks realize that Florida, for example, makes more money from their jails/institutions, than they make from tourism? That is why arresting people, whether innocent or guilty is irrelevant, it is a policeman's mandate in Florida, and many other States as well.

"The past year, the Federal Government paid out over $80 billion in compensation to all the states. Just think what that money could have done towards our crumbling infrastructure.

"In future elections, all American inmates and all American citizens will be required to vote. No political or state exceptions! Like every other civilized country in the world. Anyone or any organization preventing someone or anyone from voting will spend five years in a Federal Penitentiary.

- Police will be held accountable for their actions. Killing individuals by Police is to be eliminated. Stand Your Ground law to be appealed. NRMA politics will be eliminated. Any Politician accepting funds from the NRMA will be considered as bribery and will be arrested. The NRMA member offering these funds will also be arrested.
- Gun shows will henceforth be outlawed. Registration of firearms—all firearms—will become mandatory.
- Bring back laws and values of the common people that the Super Rich and the corrupt Politicians have taken away.
- Judges are not gods, but shall now be elected, not appointed, by the Governor.

- Lawyer's fees to be paid in installments or at the completion of their services, not up front, which discourages them from doing anything.
- The Zimmerman trial will be reopened, and proper justice will be applied. This was a clear case of a mistrial.
- Income tax for the super rich and corporations to return to what it was in the fifties and sixties. Let them pay their **fair share** of the country's expenses. The income tax laws to be amended accordingly. No gifts for the rich!
- Immediately as a top priority, start work on the American infrastructure—repairing roads, highways, bridges, dams, power stations, etc. Costs shared by federal and state governments.
- Corporations polluting our environment will henceforth be fined and forced to make amends. If they refuse, they will be closed and shut down.
- Freeze spending on Armed Forces. Maintain what we got. We do not need a larger Armed Forces. Enforce the Monroe Doctrine, protect America. Do not interfere with foreign government issues, as it is now clear we have no understanding of Foreign Affairs issues, and every venture we have entered, our soldiers die in the thousands and nothing concrete is achieved. Except we have lost our soldiers and huge

amounts of money and resources, and for what? Nothing! Expenditure on armed services is only to make the Politicians and Corporations richer, like Bush and Cheney, the Iraq War. We will, however, continue to help in humanitarian cases and in natural disasters around the world, but not in any armed combat missions.

- Expenses for lunches for friends by Politicians to be paid out of their own pockets, not from taxpayers' pockets. Retroactive for the past five years. Yes, Mr. Cantor.

- Every Corporation whose CEO makes more than $10 million, the corporation will automatically pay $5 million to the homeless and the nation's handicapped and poor via the Salvation Army or the Red Cross, all to the direction of a special appointed Board

- Natural disaster compensation to be distributed to the victims by an independent organization, not by the Governors, who at this point in time, use the money for their own slush funds and not for the assistance of the victims of natural disasters, as we have found in Alabama and New Jersey.

- An age limit be applied to all Federal Politicians and that being seventy years of age. Anyone older than that, would automatically be retired from service. An appropriate retirement package would be provided, but no lifelong pay package as now exists.

- All contracts with past and present congressmen/women are hereby void, effective and withdrawn immediately. The American people did not make these contracts with the congressmen and women. Congress made all these contracts for themselves.

- President Bush and his counterparts, Cheney, Rumsfeld, destroyed the American middle class. Millions lost the life savings, yet no one was ever blamed for it. Except that the Rich got richer as the Middle Class lost their small fortunes, which they had worked hard for. Those responsible for the infamous Bush Crash will be readdressed, and applicable charges will be forthcoming. The Middle Class deserves an answer to this Phenomena, and it should not be just brushed under the carpet so to speak. Someone needs to take the blame.

Corporations benefitting from the Crash, like the Marriott Corporation, will repay their clients accordingly. A Special Panel will review all the cases. The guilty will be brought to justice, including Bush and Cheney. No American is above the law, not even the Presidents.

Perhaps Bush and Cheney both need to be brought to task to explain just what happened and why they did absolutely nothing for the millions of Americans affected, yet their Friends, the Rich, got a giant boost in the fortunes.

- Paid public speaking engagements for Politicians will also be automatically terminated as it is part of the bribery plan, Super Rich and their puppets in the two parties have come up with. Any politician calling himself or herself an expert of Foreign Affairs is lying, as we have no experts in our past or present Government.

"Why are so many of our citizens still mourning the death of their sons and daughters? Think about it. Every venture we have entered into has cost us, the taxpayers, billions of dollars and millions of our young citizens' lives. And not one has been successful. Miraculously Bush, Cheney, etc., all got richer! Why?

"Foreign Affairs is not our business. It's high time we let foreign affairs and other nations, take care of their own business. George Bush selling Democracy is just a perfect example of how misguided our Politicians have become, as Democracy doesn't exist in the fictitious **United States**, and hasn't for quite some time.

"Corporate donations to the Political parties shall cease immediately until an appropriate board can be set up to establish a realistic donation level. The level will be determined by Congress. We all know that Corporations are polluting our land and the environment, and the Corporate donations are there to keep the two Parties silent. Not anymore!

"Too much money is wasted on frivolous and fabricating articles and propaganda that does nothing for this country. Let's deal with the issues. Let's preserve this beautiful country of ours and stop this pollution, and let's leave something for our children to appreciate and enjoy!

"The Independent Party will bring back those laws that we enjoyed when we were kids."

"We, the Independents, will introduce these major changes to our government to make this land of ours liveable again. Like I said, restrict the sale of all firearms, outlaw the gun shows/fairs, and monitor those who wish to purchase weapons through the proper channels."

"Immigrants coming to America need to understand that they *must* abide by the laws of America, not laws of their own countries! If they cannot accept our laws, don't immigrate!"

"Folks, let's not forget to serve in Congress is an honor, not a career. The Founding Fathers envisaged citizen legislators so our citizens should serve their terms, then go back home and go back to work."

"And so my friends, we have a lot of work to do to clean up this beautiful Country of ours, and our Legal Systems, but together, yes, together, we can see a new America emerge. Let's all agree that the Politicians are *not* gods living on Mount Olympus/Washington, DC. The Super Rich are *not* gods either and Corporations are *not* people.

"At this present rate, the United States will follow the Romans and fall in disgrace. The Super Rich and the Politicians have managed to take away all the values that once were the envy of the world. Now we are looked upon as another third-world country, a place you would not want to visit, for fear of being shot by some misguided individual or perhaps our trigger-happy police forces, or alternatively be arrested for some obscure charge/reason made up on the spot by our so-called law enforcement officers who have difficulty in determining whether they were holding a revolver or a Phazzer. People died, yet killers, hiding behind their badges are set free!

"In the world's eyes, America is no longer a safe place to visit, and besides, our present illustrious Government cannot decide who can visit and who cannot visit!"

Samuel stopped momentarily for a drink of cold water that Julia had handed him—a stall tactic to give the populace an opportunity to absorb what he had said.

Outside the television station, the FBI had brought in the marine teams to surround the entire studio for the duration of Samuel's declaration for the next three hours.

At this point, Samuel continued to wrap up his presentation.

"A new world will emerge after these elections. My friends, let's turn the clock back to the good old days, when there was some form of respect for each other and where we all chipped in to help the less fortunate and not pass idiotic legislation forbidding the homeless from standing under an overpass to get out of the rain! Yes, Florida!

"So what makes these Politicians, Federal and State, think that they deserve their present pay compensation packages? Only they can tell, but you already know that— sheer Greed! And no respect for the average working class American.

Thank you, America. It is now all up to you. It is your choice!

"All of this will change, rest assured, if the Independent Party can count on your support. Good night, America! Good night, my friends."

As soon as his last words rang out, Samuel was surrounded by a Navy SEAL team and quickly escorted out of the television studio to a bulletproof sedan and rushed off to an unidentified location.

It was established that the number of people that had tuned it to watch Samuel had far exceeded any previous records for the latest Super Bowl, or the arrival of the Beatles in America. It was as if the whole of America was watching! And truth be known, all of America and the world was watching!

Suddenly there was an uproar across the country. The message had reached home.

Chapter 24

The Shock to the Establishment

After listening to Samuel's platform, the Republican and Democratic Leaders, Senators, and House Representatives, and the Supreme Court Judges were all about to have heart attacks. The declaration had turned out to be a complete exposé of the Corruption in Washington, DC. All their jobs would be now in jeopardy. After the truth got out, how many of the existing Politicians would be re-elected by the now-informed, educated constituents—America's citizens?

That was the outstanding question.

Now all the Politicians, Judges, Public Prosecutors, Police Officers, in fact all those on the gravy trains had to decide whether to fight these absurd but factual allegations, or just disappear into the woodwork with their massive financial accounts, funds technically stolen from the American Public.

The "George Bush Crash" was a prime example of stealing from the Middle Class and Poor to benefit the One Percent Rich, that included George and Dick, themselves. Did they care? Not in the least!

Yes, the Time for Change, a real change, was upon the American Way of Life.

In a closed-door session, the Senior Politicians were now discussing what to do. Their gravy train had just hit a roadblock.

Part 3

The Return of
the Phoenix

Chapter 25

The Navy SEAL Operative

And so, the new chapter in Chris's life began. It was just what Chris had expected and what he was looking for. His life for the next three years was now laid out for him. He just had to meet all the challenges thrown at him. In his mind, he knew he could do it, and his physical frame was ready for the grueling training programme and tests.

When Chris finally arrived in Indianapolis at the naval academy, Jake had told him to have the Navy contact him at the FBI offices to ensure that he had immediate clearance to the program as he had just had his name changed.

With the FBI clearance, Chris was automatically admitted to the SEALS' program. Now it depended on his abilities and his passing the physical and mental tests according to the naval standards, which was not a problem for Chris as he had prepared himself for them.

Then when the other applicants and trainers saw all the scars on his back, and on his body, he was immediately nicknamed Scar out of respect for what he had already endured. No one questioned him as to how or why—that was considered as being personal, and no one else's business. Yes, he was accepted by all the other applicants and became someone that all the others looked up to. He became the team leader.

He was one of them!

During the first boot camp, Chris was briefed on the naval special operations programs. It was here that he requested to undertake the Seal PST (physical screen test), which was designed to assess the applicant's physical ability to undergo initial training. The test would be administered exactly as indicated. To become a SEAL, Chris knew he had to pass the PST Test.

He passed the PST with flying colors, and consequently he was enlisted into the SEALs program. Now the real training began. It was tough, in fact very tough, and at times, almost brutal! Many a day when he finally hit the sack, his aching body protested the rigorous training, but Chris persevered and met the challenges head-on. As the training progressed, the numbers in the group dwindled almost daily, as the physical endurance trials took their toll, but Chris's willpower and stamina met all the challenges head-on.

There were days when Chris too regretted getting involved with the grueling and painful training program, as his body ached from the stress and strain of the physical activities. But in other ways, he was grateful, as it took all his efforts and concentration to keep up with the now elite group that he was becoming a part of. To achieve the title of Navy SEAL Operative would be a landmark event and a title very few applicants ever achieved.

His muscles toned up with the daily training until he became a perfect physical male specimen, able to endure all kinds of severe conditions and situations. He learned self-defence, hand-to-hand combat, and the martial arts. He learnt how to fight with knives. He became familiar with all types of weapons of every conceivable description. He learned all about explosives and all other latest weapons available to the US forces. He trained in jungle and desert warfare. He learned survival techniques in different environments. He even spent four months at Fort Wainwright, in Alaska, taking Arctic training. He became an expert diver as he mastered diving under the various world's oceans. He became a fully trained fighting machine, able to look after himself in all types of peril and against multiple attackers.

After the two years was up, Chris had made the grade and was acknowledged as a Navy SEAL Operative, one of their best.

With all the complex and detailed training behind him, Chris was quickly transferred to the US Navy base in Broome, in Western Australia.

From Broome, the Navy SEAL teams raided the ocean pirate bases in the region, all north of Australia, like the Java Sea, Singapore Strait, and the South China Sea, the targets being based on the secret satellite photographs.

The sea raids always occurred at night, in the darkness, and always unannounced.

They came unexpectedly from the sea, and by the time they left, the pirate bases were giant infernos, lit up in flames, and all ocean-going vessels were completely destroyed. Those who were being held as hostages were rescued silently and efficiently. They too disappeared into the night. They disappeared back into the sea as the ocean's water swallowed them up.

Another base, another threat to the ocean-going vessels in the area, being eliminated, thanks to the SEALs.

He had been on several top-secret missions and assignments elsewhere as well, being flown in and then after the assignments, flown back out again. He had performed as expected, professionally, efficiently, and always within the guidelines established. Yes, he had become a Navy SEAL operative! Yes, the invisible stealth fighter that appeared mysteriously and unexpectedly and disappeared just as quickly.

Yes, he had become a Navy SEAL operative, a combat-fighting machine, one of their best. He had reached his goal, and now he felt good. For the next year, he was shipped around the world and participated in numerous assignments that, on record, never happened.

Between the raids, the SEALs got to enjoy the beautiful weather and the gorgeous deserted beaches of Western Australia, like the eighty-mile beach just south of Broome.

There, in Broome, the SEALs invariably discovered the beautiful bronzed Aussie vixens who helped them forget just what they had left behind, as they looked after their foreign visitors in the own special exclusive ways.

The SEALs certainly never complained! They also knew that their passionate relationships were all temporary as they were shipped in and out of Broome regularly on their various assignments.

Yes, the SEALs had no reasons to complain!

Chapter 26

The Return of the SEAL

After the three-year absence, first with the Navy SEALs in their training program and then as a fighting Navy SEALs Operative, Chris had been fighting the sea pirates in the Asian seas north of Australia and also being systematically shipped around the world, wherever his services were required, usually on top-level highly classified secret assignments or missions that on paper were just routine assignments and technically never happened.

After the two years of intense training and a year of a thorough training and education in espionage and stealth fighting, he was now capable of doing things that he had never ever dreamed of doing. His body was all muscle. Now one punch from Chris could easily put someone into dreamland. He could defend himself against numerous assailants and come out the winner. His self-confidence was now that of a Navy SEAL Operative, one of the toughest fighting men on the planet. Fear was not an option! That had been brainwashed out of his head.

With his dedication, he had become one of the SEAL's best Operatives, and whenever critical assignments, anywhere around the world, came up, Chris was flown in from wherever he was presently located to take the lead.

Consequently, as Broome was his home base, he flew in and out of Broome regularly, depending on the assignments around the world.

Depending on where he was located, he too had drifted into lengthy passionate, on again, off again relationships first with the persuasive erotic Oriental Kimiko Katherina Zemanova while on base and then the delectable Judy Adams, a full-bodied long-haired bronzed brunette beauty. Being quite compatible, they just enjoyed their relationship. The sex and the passion whenever they were together was great, but both knew that after his third year, he would probably just disappear, and they had accepted it.

Finally, after the three-year commitment, the time had come for Chris to return home to Kentucky as he still had one more outstanding unofficial mission to fulfill. That was his commitment to his Mother and Father to settle his account with the Baldwin organization, specifically his sadistic Uncle, the cruel and heartless Dwayne Baldwin, in Lexington, Kentucky.

But there was another issue that drew him back to Lexington.

His never-ending love affair with Kiara, his beautiful blonde Angel!

Yes, more important was the desire to reconnect with Kiara, the love of his life. Yes, without a doubt he had not forgotten her. How could he? He still loved her and had really missed her. Yes, his relationships with, Kimiko and Judy had helped, but he, Kimiko, and Judy knew their affairs were only temporary. The sex was passionate and enjoyable physically, yes, but they were meaningless mentally.

However, three years in this stage of his life was a damn long time, and anything could have happened, so he was anxious to get back to Lexington, where he had some catching up to do. Once he had finished his tour of duty, Chris was ready to head home.

He had been based out of Broome on the Western Australian Coast in the middle of nowhere. From Broome, he had been flown to Perth, where he caught the Indian-Pacific train ride across Australia, from Perth, on the Indian Ocean, across the endless Nullarbor Plains of Western Australia, to Sydney on the Pacific Ocean on the Australian East Coast, basically to give himself a little time to unwind.

Then after a week in Sydney enjoying the sights and his visits to Manly Beach and Bondi Beach, he moved on.

From Sydney, he flew back across the Pacific, first to Honolulu in Hawaii, to spend another week there, getting back to normality and just unwinding from the military routine.

Chapter 27

The Return to America

Finally, when Chris and his faithful guitar arrived back in Los Angeles, he stopped at a bar at the airport for a cold beer. Then he found a phone and immediately called Jake.

"Hey, Jake, it's Chris. I'm back in the United States again. I just arrived in LA."

"Hey, Chris, welcome home," replied Jake.

"It's good to hear your voice again, my friend," said Chris.

"Likewise, Chris, so are you finished your tour of duty, now? You heading back to Lexington again?" inquired Jake.

"Yeah, absolutely. Hey, man, we still have some unfinished business to take care of in Lexington, don't we?"

"Too right, Chris. Listen, my friend, I've got all the paperwork all ready for your return. Just for your information, and as we had previously agreed, you are now officially, with your Navy SEAL experience, an FBI secret agent and on the

FBI payroll. I have a hotel room on hold on the top floor of the Regency Hotel, which is coincidentally located right opposite the Baldwin House down on Front Street." Jake laughed.

"Perfect," agreed Chris.

"We have a car ready for you as well, a souped-up Buick Rendezvous that is somewhat indiscreet but a great machine—you'll love it! Also, let me know the time when you arrive, so I'll be able pick you up at the airport. And at that point in time, I'll be able to fill you in on all that has happened since you left."

"Great, Jake, Great!"

*   *   *

In Los Angeles, Chris arranged a connecting flight back to Nashville, and finally from Nashville, another short flight to Lexington, his hometown in his beloved Kentucky. He had really missed the bluegrass-of-Kentucky scenery and landscape and the fresh country air.

Chris spent three days in Los Angeles and Hollywood doing a little sightseeing and checking out the California blondes on the various beaches while he waited for his first-class flight back to Nashville.

Then one evening, while walking down Hollywood and Vine, suddenly Bob Seger's "Hollywood Nights" invaded his brain, and suddenly he saw his beautiful sensuous blonde beauty, Kiara, as if she were right before his eyes.

He really couldn't wait to see her again. Now in the far canyons of his mind, he already had the image of a beautiful blonde he was so anxious to see back in Lexington—yes, Kiara!

> And those Hollywood Nights
> In those Hollywood Hills
> She was looking so right
> In her diamonds and frills
> All those big city lights
> In those high rolling hills
> Above all the lights
> She had all of the skills

Yes, Kiara had all her skills, and he knew and believed that she was waiting for him and that she would show him everything again when they reconnected back in Lexington.

Late at night on the balcony of his hotel room, he looked down at the city lights of LA and dreamed of Kiara.

> Night after night, day after day, it went on and on
> Then came the morning he woke up alone
> He spent all night starring down at the lights of LA
> Wondering if he should go home
>
> (Bob Seger)

Yes, the song was somewhat out of context, but he was in LA, he was dreaming about his blonde angel, and, yes, he was definitely headed home!

Chris was headed home, all right. He still had issues to deal with.

1. Kiara, his beautiful Angel
2. The Taurus Corporation and Dwayne Baldwin

Yes, Chris was now anxious to see his Kiara again, to hold her, to kiss her again and to visit the Constellations with her again. He hoped and prayed that the three years hadn't changed their feelings for each other and that they could forget the three lost years and continue where they had left off.

Chapter 28

Back to Lexington, Kentucky

The next day, Chris had left LA and the West Coast behind him and headed back East to his destiny. Next stop was Nashville, where he was able to catch a connecting flight to Lexington within the hour.

When Chris arrived back in Lexington, he stepped out of the plane, onto the steel platform at the top of the steel stairs, he stopped momentarily, looked around. Yes, this was Lexington. In three years, nothing seemed to have changed. He then took a deep breath.

"Even the air smells as I remember it. God, it's so great to be home again," he said to himself.

As he came down the stairs, Jake was there to meet him at the small airport.

Jake hardly recognized him, as Chris had certainly put on additional weight and with muscles he never had before. Yes, he had changed, no doubt; the training with the SEALs had made a substantial difference to his body. Now he looked like a middleweight boxer, and being a fighting Navy SEAL operative, he wasn't far off that comparison, and if the facts be known, with all the new skills that he now had, he was, without a doubt, far more dangerous than a trained boxer.

With his long hair and his filled-out frame, he looked much more like a handsome rock star from the British invasion, who had just arrived in America a little too late.

"Chris, Chris! Over here," called Jake as soon as he saw Chris. Soon the two friends were hugging each other.

"Hey, man, I see you have put on a little weight and a few muscles." Jake laughed.

"And you haven't changed a bit, Jake." Chris laughed.

"Yeah, Chris, I haven't been through what you have been through in these past three years, my friend," replied Jake, pleased to touch base with Chris again. Yes, they both had one more mission to accomplish, a mission they had agreed to undertake once Chris had returned. Now was the time.

"That's the truth, for sure. I actually feel like a totally new individual, and having done what I have done, I guess I have changed completely, physically for sure, but also mentally. Jake, you know that young beat-up Eric Baldwin is long, long gone and just a pathetic memory," responded Chris.

"I feel really great, and I am very happy to be home again, and I'll be honest, I look forward to completing our assignment, and of course, reconnecting with Kiara Taylor," said Chris with a smile.

Jake smiled too. He knew about the love affair between Kiara and Chris. "Hey, I've heard she is now working at the Lexington General Hospital, in the ER, but I haven't seen her for a while," confirmed Jake.

"Let's grab your bags, Chris, then we can head over to the restaurant so I can fill you in on all that had happened here since you left, and the status of the Baldwin organization," suggested Jake.

So with his bags in hand, his guitar around his neck, he climbed into Jake's car. Jake drove him to a local restaurant, and after ordering lunch, Jake took his time as he methodically began to fill Chris in with the details of what had happened in the past three years in Lexington.

"First, let's initially and specifically deal with what the manila envelope that your father had left for US, the FBI and then on just what the Baldwins had been up to since you left," advised Jake.

"Great, Jake, I'm all ears," replied Chris.

Chapter 29

Chris's Father's Legacy

As they relaxed and each ate their respective lunches, Jake slowly began to fill Chris in on the contents of the thick manila envelope that his father had left behind in Chris's safety deposit box for the FBI.

"First, let me bring you up to date with all that happened as a result of all the documents that your father left behind. They were a great blow to Dwayne without a doubt.

"The documents were endless, and they did confirm just what we had expected. They pointed out and confirmed that many of our civic public servants City Hall, including the Mayor, were on the take—in other words, bribed. Then in our Police Force, the same thing again, including the Police Chief and the Commissioner—they were all on the Taurus payroll ledgers. Yes, they were all paid off to make life for Dwayne easy and unobstructed in Lexington and its immediate surroundings. It was no wonder none of the Baldwin gang ever got arrested for anything. That was why Dwayne really had the run of the city. He was virtually untouchable.

"But not to the FBI. We finally had the proof we had been looking for, for years," continued Jake.

"That's good to know."

"Dwayne was not a happy camper when suddenly and unexpectedly, he lost all his contacts in the Lexington City Hall and the Lexington Police Forces. Yes, all those that were getting funds from the Taurus Corporation were, in fact, all arrested."

"So my Father put the first crack in their organization!"

"He sure did."

"Great."

*   *   *

As soon as the arrests of the civil servants in City Hall got underway, Dwayne went off the deep end.

"Goddamn, son of a bitch! It must have been my damned Brother, Wayne, who leaked the information to the FBI. No one else could have done it. He was the only one who had access to our documents. He controlled all the paperwork! It must have been him. No one else could have done that!

"Now we have to recruit new people, all of which will take time and money," ranted Dwayne.

"Damn that Son of a Bitch! Getting him removed obviously was essential, but looks like he managed to screw us royally in the process. We eliminated him just a little too late. Damn it. When and how did the FBI, get all those documents?"

"No idea, boss, obviously, he had compiled them before we eliminated him! Could it have been his son, Eric? I wonder, but right after the car bomb, he was in the hospital, and we burnt their house down, so the documents obviously were not in the house. Then immediately after being released from the hospital, he was in your care. I just can't see that he had the documents. If he did, where were they? Had Wayne already given them to the FBI, I don't think so. Otherwise, they'd have been after us after the car bomb. No, I doubt it, but the pieces just don't fit!" continued Aldo, trying to piece all the information he had together. But he had no answers.

Dwayne, meanwhile, now as red as a lobster, sat in his chair drinking Jack Daniel's to calm himself down.

Next day, Dwayne's hooker wife, the obnoxious Alice, disappeared! There was an unconfirmed and rumoured report that a plastic bag that could have accommodated a dead human's body was, in fact, buried in the sand below the basement's vapor barrier and the re-bars, prior to the actual concrete pour of the six-inch slab for a basement concrete slab for a new parking garage in the city.

Her whereabouts was never established. She had just vanished, her body never found.

Then when Dwayne heard about the Police Force and the arrests of the Police Chief and the

Commissioner, he went absolutely berserk and had to be sedated by Aldo.

"Hey, Boss, let's cool it for the next while, or the FBI will be in to arrest us too! If they have enough documents to arrest our contacts in City Hall, including the Mayor and also in the Police Force, including the Police Chief and the Commissioner himself, then they probably have enough to come after us as well, so, Boss, be careful what you say or do for the next while, or we'll all be in trouble."

*   *   *

"Chris, your father's 'borrowed' documents really set Dwayne in a whirl. The Governor and the State National Guard came in and cleared out the Municipal Offices, including the Mayor, and also the Lexington Police Department, including the Police Chief and the Commissioner, and all those that were on the Baldwin's payroll as per the documents.

"Well, it took almost a year to clean house, but I am sure Dwayne has some new recruits at City Hall and in the Police Department again who are prepared to take the risk for a few extra bucks, which is typical in today's society. But understand-ably whoever they are at this point, they are play-ing it very cool.

"So anyway, your Father certainly did us a great service in providing us with those documents, but regretfully He and your Mother paid the price, and you escaped by the skin of your teeth.

"So it's now up to us to complete this mission, Chris, so let's meet tomorrow morning, once you are booked in, and let's look at what we can do to get started on just what we need to do to put the Baldwins out of commission and close down their operations completely.

"Here are your keys to your Buick Rendezvous parked in the hotel's parking lot. Check into to your room and check out all the various gadgets you asked for. Then have a meal in the hotel's dining room, all of which goes on the FBI tab. You are now an undercover agent and under the FBI.

"We'll meet again for breakfast at 8.00 a.m. Get a good night's sleep. Tomorrow we'll begin our final assignment with the Baldwin organization."

"Great, Jake, I appreciate all that you have done. Yes, we have an assignment to complete—bring this city out of the grips of the Taurus and Baldwin organizations."

"You know, Chris, this was a quiet, peaceful city, and even under the control of your grandfather, it was still a nice place to live, but when he passed away and Dwayne took over and bought the police force, things really changed around here.

"You and I will bring back the old good times again and get rid of this virus that had infected this town of Lexington.

"Oh, by the way, Allen asked me to tell you the next time I talked to you that Midnight won the Kentucky Derby last year. Also, that Midnight's Owner has a bonus for you, for your contribution in training Midnight."

"No kidding! That's great! What a remarkable horse! He really was a champion." Chris laughed. "I'm happy he came through."

Chapter 30

The Taurus Corporation and the Baldwin Organization

Next morning, Jake met with Chris again for breakfast to make sure he was all settled into his hotel room and with all the applicable surveillance equipment that Chris had asked for.

After their full egg-and-bacon breakfast, they got down to business.

"As I told you yesterday, we have set you up in this here Regency Hotel on State Street, right beside or opposite Baldwin house, the old brick office building that they still own and have occupied now for years. The main entrance to the Baldwin house actually faces the hotel, and you have a room up on the top eighth floor, perfectly positioned, so you'll be able to see all the activity that goes on in that building from your window. In your room, we have in place a voice pickup screen and all kinds of surveillance, audio and video receivers as per your request," advised Jake.

"Great, it'll take me several days to stake out the Baldwin house, but with the two external steel fire escapes, they have made my work so much easier for me," replied Chris.

"Well, being such on old building, I'm sure their security system is old school, one that I'll be able to disarm in no time. After I establish all their entry points, I'll be able to bug the telephone system and all the various offices as well with both audio and video receivers.

"Oh, their parking lot, which they also do own, is that vacant parcel of land on the south side of their building. The Baldwin house has no vehicular entry anywhere."

"Good, even better, I am sure there are large duct shafts running through the building where we'll be able to place all our little bugs." Chris laughed.

The fact was, the old brick office building had been bought years ago by Chris's grandfather, and when Dwayne took it over, being such a cheapskate, he never upgraded the facility to modern electrical standards, telecommunication-wise or relative to the security standards.

As the Baldwin House was known by all the locals as being connected to the Mafiosi business and activities, so for safety's sake, most people stayed clear of the facility.

Chris found that he had a clear view of the Baldwin house from his window on the eighth floor, so he could monitor exactly what happened on a daily basis and get photographs of all those entering the facility, including Dwayne and Aldo, his right-hand man.

From his observations, it was clear that the building was not patrolled by anyone at any time. Having around-the-clock security cost money, and Dwayne, in his naive state of mind, didn't bother. No one dared to trespass in the Baldwin Building.

In essence, the Shadow's explorations were easy, and with his Navy SEAL training, Chris had the run of the building. He could virtually observe what was going on in almost all the various offices, including Aldo's and Dwayne's own offices.

Chris had adopted the nickname "the Shadow" that his teammates at boot camp and on the Navy SEAL bases where he had been based on his tours had bestowed on him. It was a name he had grown used to.

With Jake's contacts and access to the latest surveillance equipment, audio and video, soon Jake had brought Chris up to date with all that Dwayne was now up to.

As soon as Jake had supplied Chris with all the applicable surveillance equipment, Chris, with his espionage experience, over several nights, had the Baldwin Building all wired for audio and video throughout, without Dwayne even having any idea what Chris had done.

Jake also provided Chris a voice frequency analyser that could distinguish people's voice frequencies, and by a twist on the dial, the reader could simulate anyone's voice over the phone. Chris intended to use the gadget to get Dwayne and Alice fighting each other. He of course was unaware initially that Dwayne had already eliminated Alice.

Chris had staked out the building on all four sides, and the adjacent parking lot, giving himself a clear picture of the Baldwin House.

With Jake's help, they identified the photographs of those entering the building—the capo, the soldiers, etc.

It was Chris's intension to enter the Baldwin house after hours, disarm the antiquated alarm system, and implant all the various telephone bugs and all the miniature surveillance equipment, which he would hide as best as he could in locations where no one would expect them to be.

By monitoring them daily, Chris and Jake / FBI could then easily determine the Baldwin's daily activities.

Next Chris checked all the possible access points, grilles, vents, the mechanical duct vents on the roof which he found were never sealed off or locked off with some form of metal grilles. The building, in essence, was totally open to any form of vandalism; only the reputation of the Baldwin Corporation kept vandals away, as no one wanted to mess with them.

This was just perfect for the Shadow, as he almost waltzed through the building, leaving miniature audio and video sensors all over the place. Some vertical exhaust ducts running vertical down in the middle of the building were large enough to allow a person on a nylon rope ladder to travel down the vertical ducts to various offices and to listen in on various meetings and conversations.

Through the metal grilles in the walls, someone inside the ducts could readily see the occupants in the various offices, including Dwayne private office as well, without anyone knowing.

In another duct shaft, Chris discovered a private plush lounge with an actual large bed in it. It was where Dwayne and Aldo were often entertained by local professional hookers.

So Chris was now virtually able to establish just what the capos were being ordered to do by Aldo and Dwayne just by listening in on and recording their conversations. Chris also noted that his father had been replaced by another Italian individual named Enrico, who obviously catered totally to Dwayne.

Chapter 31

The Constellations Revisited

It was late spring; the weather was great, and it was getting warmer day by day. The Wind Crest Hills Thoroughbred Horse Estate was coming alive. Even the horses were frolicking about. The air was actually smelt fresh, clean, and invigorating.

But there was another issue, a more pleasant issue, that Chris had to deal with—Kiara!

Yes, for three years Chris had dreamt about her every night and imagined just how their passionate reunion would be, chasing each other through the various Constellations. Yes, now he was anxious to find out just what had happened to Kiara and Alycia. Yes, they had promised to wait until he returned, but at their young ages, many things could have happened, and one could have met all kinds of new and different and exciting individuals.

Kiara, in reality, had expected to be involved in various affairs with others but with meaningless sex—male and female, it didn't matter—but not to the degree that she had experienced in that first year at Uni.

But that was now all over and something in the past, but in some ways, she relished those experiences which she had in truth enjoyed, but she was also convinced that those experiences had made her a much sexier young lady and more experienced to look after Chris when he returned.

Chris too had been entertained by the Oriental beauty Kimiko, and yes, those bronzed beauties on the Broome Beaches, but in his own mind, they were all only temporary acquaintances. He still had a date with his one and only, Kiara, at the end of his Tour of Duty.

Today was the day of reconciliation and the day both he and Kiara, and in many ways Alycia too, had been waiting for. Today they would discover, whether the magic of their union was still there. Did they still have that passion for each other, and did they really have a future together?

So Chris climbed into his Buick Rendezvous and drove out to the Wind Crest Hills Thoroughbred Horse Estate that he knew so well. His mind was clouded, full of expectations. What surprizes had Fate arranged, he would find out soon enough.

Alycia had just stepped out of her mist shower and stood there staring at herself in front of the floor-to-ceiling mirror in all her naked voluptuous glory, as she wrapped a towel around her long blonde hair.

Then unconsciously, lost in a daydream, she ran her exploring fingers over her firm full sensuous breasts, tweaking her sensitive protruding rosy red nipples, just as Chris had done for her the night she stood in for Kiara, but that was three years ago.

Suddenly and unexpectedly the door bell range and immediately brought her out of her daydream.

"God, with Allen away again, this time in California, who could that be?" she wondered. She quickly took her terry towel dressing gown and wrapped it around her gorgeous body as she headed for the front door.

When Alycia opened the door, holding the dressing gown tight around herself, she uttered almost automatically, "Good morning. How can I help you?"

She looked at the young handsome hunk of a man staring at her with that great big familiar smile on his face and those piercing blue eyes she had never forgotten, not saying a word, and was caught completely by surprise. Then suddenly, something clicked inside her head! It was him. He was back!

Yes, she knew this handsome man. Yes, she knew him all right. Then when her brain had sorted out the visual appearance of this stranger and recognized him, she just about fainted. She stood there dumbfounded as she realized who it was!

"Chris? Oh my god, Chris, Baby, Chris! Oh my God, you're back!" she screamed as she immediately reached for him. She pulled him inside and closed and locked the door as she wrapped her dressing gown–clad body around him as her lips pressed hard against his in a long passionate French–style kiss.

"Oh my God, Chris, oh my God, it is really you. I cannot believe this. You are back, you are back! How wonderful," she uttered almost hysterically. "Somehow you look different, but those eyes and that smile, they are still the same! God, this is really great!" she cried enthusiastically and so excitedly, virtually jumping up and down on the spot.

"God, I have to call Kiara immediately! She'll have a fit. She'll go crazy, I know it, and then she'll be on her way here like a flash. She'll been waiting for your return, like every day. She'll need to see you as soon as possible, I know it, and you can count on it!" rambled Alycia.

"Oh my God, this is going to be such a special day, without a doubt, exactly just what Kiara and I have been waiting for. And Allen's away for a week, perfect!" she said to herself.

Suddenly Alycia pulled the towel from her head and shook her long hair free and loose, then surprisingly the front of her dressing gown opened up, exposing the front of her voluptuous body to Chris, as Alycia allowed the gown to slide to the floor.

"Oh my God! Come on in, Chris, come in, come in," she said excitedly as she wrapped her naked body around him as she passionately kissed him again, then dragged him into her bedroom. Chris's hands had already found her gorgeous full breasts. He fondled them somewhat aggressively.

Alicia didn't mind at all. In the bedroom, they kissed each other so passionately as Alycia began stripping Chris. Alycia already knew that he was already fully aroused.

"Before we do anything, I have to call Kiara. She really is dying to see you again and to passionately love you again and to re-establish the relationship that the two had, and hopefully you both will allow me to be the icing on the cake again." Alycia laughed.

Then Alycia pulled free and immediately grabbed her phone and called Kiara at the hospital.

"Hey, Mom, What's up?"

"Honey, listen, a strange very handsome young man came to the door a few minutes ago, looking for you, looking like one of the British Invasion Rock Gods from the sixties, long hair, the build of a middleweight prize fighter. God, it was Chris. He's back! Better than ever, Hun! You are really gonna love him now. I guarantee it."

Kiara gave out a little scream. "I'm on my way, Mom," responded Kiara. "Just finished my shift. I'll be right over. Don't let him out of your sight and don't let him go anywhere! Keep him occupied till I get there." Kiara laughed joyfully.

"Don't worry, he's not going anywhere. He's here anxiously waiting for you, so hurry," responded Alycia as she continued systematically removing his clothing as she finally had him stripped him naked, all ready for Kiara. Alycia already had him in her hand, stroking him.

Then Kiara smiled and whispered softly so only Alycia could hear, "Hey, Mom, warm him up for me," she said, almost laughing. Seconds later she raced to her car. This was the day that would decide their future, and she knew it.

Alycia and Chris continued making out passionately as Chris continued to fondle Alycia's delicious breasts and her soft, tender naked sensuous body. Alycia was almost ready to attack Chris herself. She too was so aroused as well.

"Gotta go, emergency at home!" Kiara cried. Fortunately, her shift was virtually over, so her leaving created no problems, as the next Doctor was already there to take over.

Then she raced to her car and headed home as fast as the traffic lights permitted. Meanwhile Alycia had already stripped Chris naked, advised him that Kiara was on her way and, that she was to warm him up for her, so instantly she pushed him down onto her bed. Chris was already aroused, so Alycia instantly took him in her mouth and began to perform fellatio on him enthusiastically.

Minutes later, the front door opened and closed almost instantly. By the time Kiara reached the bedroom, she was already topless, her gorgeous breasts swaying from side to side, only wearing her briefs, which disappeared quickly. Alicia moved aside. She allowed Kiara to immediately straddle him and instantly impale herself on him. Seconds later their lips were locked together as the frantic action started. Alicia was thrilled, and Kiara was virtually out of her mind as she bounced up and down on her long-lost lover! Her lover was back, yes, he was back, ready to continue their love affair where they had left off. Chris was lost in the blur of sexual activity over the balance of the afternoon as Kiara and Alycia shared him completely.

This was the reunion they had all hoped for, and they knew this was going to last until the next morning, only stopping for some dinner and to catch their breaths.

Three years later, it was very obvious their love for each other was still there, now stronger than ever.

Alycia ordered in some Chinese food as she didn't want to miss anything. Then after stopping for some food and drinks, they hurriedly caught the express flight to the Cassiopeia Constellation, where they chased each other all night long until the sunrise finally forced them back to earth, basically to recover and to get some sleep.

They knew they would never forget that night. The enthusiasm in all three of them was simply amazing. Yes, the love affair of Kiara and Chris was stronger than ever, and they knew they would be together now for a long, long, long time.

Kiara and Chris now had their answers. Yes, they were meant to be together, and the foundation of the love they had built before was still solid, and now lying in each other arms, the smiles were on their faces. They were happy and oh so content and satisfied, as all three of them slept.

Chapter 32

The Colombian Drug Shipment

One night, as soon as it was dark again, Chris again made his appearance as the Shadow, and in the darkness, he crossed the Street to the Baldwin House. There on the northern steel fire escape stairs, he slowly, silently, he made his way up onto the roof. Confirming that the roof was vacant and no one was present, he again made his way to the vertical duct shaft, where he lowered himself down the nylon rope ladder to where Dwayne's office was located.

He arrived just as one of their capos and one soldier came into Dwayne's office. The conversation was related to tomorrow night's private aircraft delivering their quarterly supply of drugs, from Colombia, specifically some Heroin , but also the major shipment of the expensive Columbian Cocaine.

Unofficially it was supposed to be a shipment of exotic blends of Colombian coffee beans for Manuel

Olivetti, a local retailer, obviously in cohorts with Dwayne. As soon as Chris heard the word *drugs*, he immediately recorded all the informative conversation.

The private jet was supposed to land at 8:00 p.m. in the dark as it had done so many times before, so no one would suspect anything.

Chris called Jake right away when he got back to his hotel room. They agreed to meet next morning to review the situation so they could prepare to intercept the shipment at the airport.

" Probably, there had been coffee beans in their initial shipment, when the airport's Customs had checked the shipment, but obviously, the goods had changed on the subsequent shipments to drugs." Suggested Jake.

By the morning Jake had already checked with the airport's Customs, who confirmed that the first shipment they had checked was, in fact, coffee beans, but there had been nine other shipments since. It was assumed they too were coffee beans, but where they?

Not likely. The drugs provided Dwayne the major portion of his monthly operating capital, and a hefty bonus, income to his already substantial bank account, which his Father and Grandfather had built up over the years!

The conversation Chris had overhead obvious put some doubt in the FBI's minds. "Perhaps the first shipment was coffee, but knowing Dwayne, I can almost guarantee the rest of the shipments were drugs," said Jake. "Well, tomorrow night we will find out. Good work, Chris. This is exactly what we wanted."

The next night the FBI agents were waiting, and most were dressed in maintenance overalls, so when the private plane arrived and pulled into a darkened area of the small airport, Jake and Chris sat in Jake's Jeep and watched in silence as all the packages were loaded onto the movable cart. The Baldwin tuck had already pulled up beside the private plane ready to receive the goods, but unexpectedly the ground crew this time moved the goods into the airports warehouse instead of the customary waiting Baldwin truck.

Manuel and Aldo protested vehemently, but the FBI were now in procession of the goods, and the FBI agents were now carefully unloading the packages and one by one. There were no coffee beans, only packets of white powder.

"Strange, these don't look like coffee beans to me, gentlemen," commented Agent Phillips, as Jake and Chris listened in on the conversation with smiles on their faces.

"Look, I know nothing about these drugs. We were expecting coffee beans."

"Did I say anything about drugs, Agent Monroe?"

"No, sir, you said nothing about drugs."

"Yeah right!" suggested Phillips, the FBI agent in charge. "And who were your customers for the coffee beans here in Lexington, Aldo?"

"Obviously, Manuel," replied Aldo.

"Right, then tomorrow, Manuel, we want to see all your receipts for your sales of all the coffee beans for the past nine shipments, defining the types of beans, the quantities, and to who you sold them to. Okay?"

There was no answer from Manuel. Obviously there were no receipts, and he knew it.

"Aldo, any ideas?" Agent Phillips laughed.

Then turning to his two other agents, he said, "Take Aldo and Manuel down to the station and book them up for supposed drug trafficking. They can call their lawyers in the morning. We'll take care of these drugs."

"Yes, sir," responded the FBI officers as they handcuffed both Manuel and Aldo and drove them down to FBI headquarters.

So Manuel was arrested immediately, as was Aldo. The Baldwin truck quickly disappeared. Aldo claimed he too was expecting coffee beans, which had been the usual cargo, something had obviously gone wrong and their contacts in Colombia had sent them the wrong cargo.

When Luigi, the capo, called Dwayne at Home, Dwayne went off the deep end. Needless to say, he immediately drove down to the FBI station, picking up his lawyer in the process, demanding that Aldo be released immediately, as the contents of the shipment had obviously been switched without them knowing, and Aldo was a victim of the circumstance.

"See us in the morning, Mr. Baldwin, and we suggest you bring your lawyer again, and not until bail has been set, and that won't be until after ten tomorrow at the earliest. Besides, we still have not had our interrogation conversation with either Manuel or Aldo at this point, and that won't happen until tomorrow, when Jake comes in. Good night, Mr. Baldwin," responded the officer at the front desk calmly, actually enjoying giving Mr. Baldwin the gears.

Knowing there was nothing he could do at that point, Dwayne and his lawyer left the station, mad as hell.

Suddenly now he had a major problem. His supply of drugs to his regular customers for the next three months had suddenly and unexpectedly dried up. Now he had to find some drugs quickly to satisfy his customers, or loose them to another supplier or another source.

Yes, this was exactly what Jake and the Shadow had hoped for. This was the beginning of the downfall of the Baldwin organization.

This was the first time the Baldwin organization had been caught importing illegal drugs into Lexington from Colombia.

Dwayne was convinced that someone had snitched and advised the FBI, but who? Aldo? No. Not Aldo, he knew better. One of the capos? Perhaps! Alice? She knew about the shipment as well.

Suddenly Aldo now had to eat some humble pie. He had to find some replacement drugs and the quantities he needed—and quickly.

When he called New York, they just laughed at him. "Look, you arrogant Son of a Bitch, now that you got a problem, you suddenly are Mr. Nice Guy. Get lost, buddy!" was New York's reply.

Dwayne suddenly heard a barrage of suggestions as to what he should do and then the continual laughter before New York Hung up the phone!

New York loved it and took full advantage of Dwayne's dilemma, and since Dwayne had not treated New York with any respect before, he was finding his arrogance was not paying off any dividends. He got no help from New York. The same response came from Miami and Los Angeles. The Colombian source had just cut him off, so Dwayne was about to lose his drug customers. That was a real crisis for Dwayne, as the drugs were his major source of income.

So who was the snitch? Dwayne had no idea.

Someone had tipped off the FBI, knowing that the shipment was tonight and exactly at what time and where. But who? Dwayne wouldn't be able to talk to Aldo or Manuel until after 10:00 a.m. tomorrow at the earliest, to see if they could establish who had snitched. But that really was the minor problem now. The real issue was, where would he, could he, get enough drugs to satisfy his customers? That was the problem. Furthermore, this seriously really cut into his three-month operating cash flow as well.

Dwayne had a problem—he needed money to buy drugs on the open market. Even if it cost him, it was important to keep his regular customers and keep them happy! If he missed a delivery, his customers would disappear, he knew that, and that affected his cash flow big time.

Chapter 33

The Senator's Visit

One night again as Chris was moving in his stealth mode through the Baldwin Building, he stumbled on a very interesting conversation right again in Dwayne's office.

"Hey, Senator Adams, so good to hear from you again. What can we do for you this time?" There was a slight pause. "Can't talk about it over the phone? Fine. Why don't you and the House Reps come to Lexington and meet with us here in my office. I'm sure we can work out a deal for you to get rid of this pest. We always look after repeat Customers." Then after another pause, "Yes, Senator Adams, we understand. He is becoming a real problem for all you guys in Washington, DC." Dwayne laughed out loud as he was obviously hearing more comments from the Senator.

Chris was no fool. As soon as he heard "Senator Adams," he immediately turned on his tape recorder and recorded the conversation.

"Yes, Senator, next Thursday at 8:00 p.m. in my office will be just fine. You already know where we are located. Yes, yes that is correct. I know you and Dad had many dealings before, and we have had our share too. Look, not to worry, we'll take care of business as we usually do. Look, Senator, fly in on your private plane at around 7:30 p.m. It will be dark by that time. We'll pick you all up at the Airport, and we will drive you and your Associates to our office," confirmed Dwayne. "No one will know that you've been here at all, I promise you."

"Yes, okay, Senator. See you next week," concluded Dwayne with a great big smile on his face. This was exactly what he was looking for, cash, millions to fill the gap with the loss of the income from the Baldwin's seized drugs. So he had to assassinate Bateman, big deal, just another body. Dwayne chuckled as things were becoming to look brighter again. Dwayne still hadn't resolved the drug issue, but he was still convinced someone had tipped the FBI off, but who? He had no clue.

*   *   *

Chris immediately called Jake and played back the tape.

"Jake, guess what? I do believe we've hit the jackpot! Dwayne is meeting with Senator Adams and two House Representatives here in Lexington, in Dwayne's Office at 8:00 p.m. next Thursday."

"No kidding. Fantastic. I think this is what we have been waiting for, Chris. Great work man, great work."

*   *   *

Chris and Jake were sitting silently up on the roof of the Baldwin Building, totally hidden in the shadows, their stun revolvers beside them, in case they were interrupted, and hooked up to the audio and visual sensors. Jake was viewing the miniature monitor, and Chris listening in as well. Jake easily picked up the players, Senator John Adams from Texas and House Representatives George Oldman from Louisiana and Gerry Wilson from Georgia.

"Senator Adams, pleased to see you again," said Dwayne with his typical sneer as he poured himself and Aldo a couple of glasses of bourbon without offering the Senator or his Associates, George Oldman, and Gerry Wilson, the House Representatives, a glass. Being social was not Dwayne's forte. He was his arrogant self. Then as he took a sip of the bourbon, he looked at the Senator and smiled.

"Okay, Senator, so what is the nature of your business this time? What exactly do you what us to do?" asked Dwayne, already knowing full well what was on the agenda.

"Well, Mr. Baldwin, you already appreciate we, the Federal and the State Politicians of the great Country of ours, have an immediate problem!"

"Mr. Samuel Bateman, the Independent Senator who is not surprisingly making all you corrupt Federal and State senators and House Representatives a little nervous, right?" said Dwayne, almost laughing.

"Yes, you could say that. He is absolutely threatening closing down our gravy train, our existing lifestyle."

"Shame, Senator! Frankly you guys, the One Percent, have had it far too easy for far too long. Do no work, money for life. Perhaps he is right. You guys are more corrupt than we are, but at least we acknowledge that we are. Perhaps we all should support him and save the country a hell of a lot of money from you leeches."

"Yeah, well..."

"Okay, Senator, so much for the humor. You want us to eliminate Senator Samuel Bateman... Right?"

"Precisely!"

"It will cost you!"

"We realize that, but we are prepared to pay."

"Well, Senator, we can certainly accommodate you and do that, but why not contact the Taipan, the famous hitman? He virtually guarantees all his hits."

"We tried, but he refuses to work in the States. Says we cannot be trusted, and besides, he supports Senator Bateman! Can you imagine?"

"Then what about our Cousins up in New York?"

"We approached them too, but they are laughing. They are actually hoping that Bateman gets in.

They are loving it too! But regardless, if by a fluke Bateman was to get in and the Independents took control of the Government, our Political System would face total chaos, and if he were to pass the Offshore Assets Bill that he is talking about, there would be serious consequences for the Super Rich," responded Senator Adams. "That is why Senator Bateman needs to disappear, and the sooner, the better."

"Okay, okay. We get the picture, Senator. I never realized just how scared you guys really are, aren't you? This is great! I love it! Finally, Samuel Bateman has created a stir and touched the nerve of the Super Rich. Suddenly all the Millionaires, Billionaires, and specifically all the Politicians are all running scared.

"It's about time! You slime have been raping this Country and the Average Americans for far too long. Perhaps I too should tell you guys to fly a kite too, but my business is money—home-grown money!"

"Now please appreciate, for us to eliminate Bateman, specifically now that America has finally seen the light, it will cost you big bucks, especially now with all the added security around him."

"You can bet the FBI will have a tight web around him, so to get close to him will not be easy, but since you guys are so anxious to get rid of him, it will cost you $ 10M...$5M deposit, balance upon completion of the assignment. We do nothing until the $5M is deposited into our account. You will then have only two business days to deliver the balance, once it is confirmed that Samuel Bateman is dead. If for some unknown reason, we do not get our money, we will start eliminating the Leaders of the Democrats and the Republicans in our time frame. So we suggest no double crosses.

"Let's face it, you guys are all accessible to us, and so are your families. Nothing personal, Senator. As I said, we are in the business for only one thing...Money!"

"That's a hell of a lot of money, Mr. Baldwin, and specifically without any guarantees," responded the Senator.

"Listen, Senator, that's a risk you take! How much would each of you Fat Cats lose if he were to cut off your offshore assets? In fact, the $10M is just a pittance of what you guys have stolen from the American People and what you would lose."

"Listen, talk to your Pharmaceutical CEO, who earns $ 124M yearly plus benefits. Get him and your Corporations to contribute to the fund." Dwayne laughed. "So don't give me any of your crap about $10m being a lot of money."

The Senator and House Representatives kept quiet and said nothing more.

"Okay...when do you want this to happen?" questioned Dwayne as he now realized he hated these three scumbags; they were no better than himself.

"ASAP," responded the Senator.

"Okay, Aldo, give the Senator our Bank Account Number. Remember it's the Chase Manhattan Bank Account 99567899."

"Sure, Mr. Baldwin, I'll get the applicable documents," acknowledged Aldo.

"Thank you, Dwayne," said Chris to himself. Jake just sat there, concentrating.

"So are we in Agreement with the $10M, Senator, or not, or are you just wasting my time?" sneered Dwayne.

"Yeah, we're in agreement," replied the Senator, who now realized he hated the gangster, Dwayne Baldwin, as well, but he had very few options left for him. Yes, he had no choice. He needed someone like Dwayne to take care of business, and if they could get rid of Samuel Bateman for $10M, he knew that would be a bargain! That would ensure that the Independent Movement/Party would crumble and immediately disappear from the Presidential race. Without Samuel Bateman, there is no question, there would be No Independent's Party!

"Okay, leave it with me for two weeks. We'll have to work out a schedule and also determine what Mr. Bateman's schedule is, find out where he is going to be and where he is planning to go."

"Then we will give you some dates as to when and where it could happen. We also have to determine just how much protection he has from the FBI."

"Okay, we will wire you the deposit money tomorrow morning."

"Good, then we will go to work. Then you actually believe this guy has a chance?"

The way the polls are going, there could be a real shock to the Establishment. A real awakening. It will change everything. I cannot even imagine what will happen. America won't be the same!"

Chris and Jake smiled. They had the whole conversation, all on tape. Jake Sanders finally had what he needed!

"Looks like the FBI has to basically create a shield around Samuel Bateman, and a heavy solid shield, as unknowingly Samuel Bateman holds the future of America in his hands," said Jake.

"It certainly appears that way," responded Chris. "Looks like the existing Politicians are really running scared and consequently are prepared to spend a lot of their donated Corporate Funds to make sure that their lifestyle and their million-dollar benefits plans did not disappear."

Yes, the Government's Politicians themselves were now the problem.

Now the CIA and the FBI as well and special Army and Navy units were being brought in to make sure that the Independent Candidates were not being threatened.

The major problem was that the Baldwin Organization was only one group. Without a doubt, there could be many other groups, many separate individuals, all armed to the teeth, who, for a big pay day could attempt to take out Samuel Bateman when he least expected it. Yes, so many others could try to eliminate Samuel as well, and obviously for their own benefits...Money!

Without a doubt, Samuel was now a marked man with an invisible target superimposed on his chest and back. The FBI now, with the latest information, had a specific team assembled giving Samuel Bateman protection coverage 24/7, wherever he was located or wherever he traveled.

Yes, the existing Politicians were now running scared, as suddenly the Independent Candidates were being registered in virtually all the States. The Leaders of the Republicans and the Democrats couldn't believe it. Who was bankrolling the Independents? Where did they get the money?

Surprisingly the existing Democratic Senator and House Representative in Alaska declared themselves as Independents, so consequently at this point, the Democrats had no Candidates running in Alaska. Similar situations were occurring in other States as well. Many of the Politicians saw the writing on the wall, as they too switched Parties, all believing that the Independents would sweep the Election, specifically after the "Hitman Controversy," and it would be a better option for them to be a Senator or House Representative in the new Government, with a decent job than an unemployed ex-Politician from the corrupt Government. Yes, they would not have the gravy-train benefits, but they would have a decent-paying job.

It was now very evident that the Popular Vote was headed for the Independents, and if the new predictions became through, there could be three Parties in Congress for the first time in American History, with the Independents actually holding a majority of seats in both the Senate and the House of Representatives, with the Democrats and Republicans trailing way behind.

Then the next President could really well be Samuel Bateman, the Leader of the Independents.

This Election was going to bring the Country back into the hands of the People, not the Super Rich, where it was now. If Bateman did become President and he did carry out his promises, then the structure of the American Politics would have taken a giant step toward turning the Government back to where it was supposed to be—"by the People and for the People."

Chapter 34

The FBI Steps in

The incriminating tape of Texas Senator John Adams's meeting with Dwayne Baldwin was reviewed by FBI Headquarters, who immediately issued Arrest Warrants for Senator John Adams, George Oldman (Louisiana), and Gerry Wilson (Georgia).

The FBI verified that Senator Adams and his two accompanying House Representatives had returned to Washington.

Early next morning, the Senator tried twice to wire Dwayne Baldwin the $5 million to his Account, but found that the transfer had been blocked.

"Damn, what the hell is going on? Why is the transfer blocked?" wondered the Senator.

Just then there was a knock on his door, as his Personal Secretary, Nancy Osborne, rushed in, "I tried to stop them, Senator, but they insisted on coming in. They claimed they are from the FBI."

Suddenly a cold sweat covered the Senator's body!

"Yes, Senator, we are definitely from the FBI, and you, Sir, are hereby under arrest. Please understand that anything you say can be used against you in a Court of Law, so it is advisable you keep your mouth shut!" stated the arresting officer for the FBI.

"What's the meaning of this outrage? What am I charged with?" inquired the Senator nervously.

"We think you know only too well, Senator. Please understand that the House Representatives George Oldman and Gerry Wilson are both under arrest as well. As we have said, we suggest you say nothing and let your lawyer answer for you. So much for your trip to Lexington!"

With that statement, the Senator fainted and collapsed onto the floor!

Handcuffed like a criminal, the Senator and the two House Representatives were all led out of their respective offices.

The five-million-dollar transfer the next morning to the Baldwin Account was blocked, so technically, the Hitman was not engaged, but this was only one instance. The question was, were there other organizations that had been engaged by the Republican and Democratic Delegates prior to their meeting in Lexington?

When the news reached the White House and Congress, the outcome of these coming Elections was almost sealed. The American Public was furious. All donations from the Public ceased, and the Corporations also stopped all donations to both

Parties, as they didn't want to be associated with the corruption in the Political Parties.

Whether the others in the Republican and Democratic Senators caucus and House Representatives knew about the hiring of the Hitman to take out Samuel Bateman was not clear, but it was certain that the Party Leaders, both Republican and Democratic Parties, knew! The fact was that they never expected to get caught. Suddenly the American Politicians themselves and corrupt Corporations were the Nation's Enemies. not some Foreign Radical Powers, but local Americans themselves.

The Media wasted no time reporting the arrests of the senior Republican Senator, one of the prominent Republican Leaders, and the two House Representatives, one Republican and the other a Democrat.

The connection to Lexington and the Baldwin Organization was quickly made, giving the media ample opportunity to speculate exactly what the meeting in Lexington had been about. The Nation was totally shocked.

Samuel was shocked, as Jake and Chris actually played back the audio and the video tapes to Samuel personally. Samuel now realized that the Republicans and the Democrats were now desperate, and in a way he was encouraged. This meant that his message had reached the American people.

This was a sign that perhaps the Independents were making great grounds/advances, and yes, perhaps the American People had finally come to their senses and now was the time finally to reclaim their own country from these Fat Cats and corrupt Corporations.

Chapter 35

The President's Address

When the news reached the White House, the incumbent present President went absolutely berserk, out of his mind. This was the last straw!

Suddenly the nation's President, with an Executive Order, cut in on regular programming and went on air, live, vehemently condemning the action taken by the leadership of the Republican and Democrats Parties.

"My fellow Americans, today we all heard some very depressing and deplorable news. I myself am totally embarrassed that our elected representatives could stoop so low to actually attempt to engage a hit man, totally outside our country's laws, to assassinate another Politician, in an attempt to save their own Political seats in Congress, for the upcoming Election."

"If this is what our present Government Politicians have become, then I personally endorse Samuel Bateman and his Independent platform."

"As we all know, in the past eight years—no, in the past *sixteen* years, our Government has achieved nothing as the two-party system is always locked, and no one is prepared to make a decision, but all the bills that have been passed have been bills to benefit themselves and the American One Percent, the Corporations...nothing, and I stress, nothing for the American People."

"This action is incredible and highlights the corruption that presently exists within this Government! This is not acceptable, and rest assured this will not be tolerated. Forthwith as Commander in Chief, I am declaring Martial Law and consequently Congress is hereby closed until the election. With Executive Orders, I will see us through to the Election.

"I would resign right now, but regretfully I do not know which way the Vice President, nor the Speaker of the House are leaning, and I don't want anyone muddying the waters any further. Are they a party to the Conspiracy by the corrupt Corporations and the corrupt Politicians that presently sit in Congress, I honestly do not know.

"Thus, as Commander in Chief, in an unprecedented move, I have just issued an executive Presidential Order dismissing the Supreme Court until a new one can be selected by the people to replace these bought judges, and the closure of Congress until the new election. All paychecks are hereby on hold until after the election.

"Frankly, my fellow Americans, this truly is a deplorable and a disgusting situation we are presently facing. What ever happened to Democracy? Obviously, it does not exist any longer in America. The question is, How long has this been going on? And how long has it been covered up?

"For example, with reference to President Bush's Crash, the Rich got richer while millions of our American Citizens lost their hard-earned life savings, and to this day the entire event has been covered up and brushed under the carpet, so to speak! To this day, no one has been arrested or indicted for this massive theft for the American Middle Class funds! No one!

"This issue will be addressed again, and those guilty will be brought to justice. No one is above the law, not even the President. And this time there will be no pardons issued. But not under this Government that has covered up the issue up until now. As Samuel, has pointed out, the time of Reckoning has come.

"Obviously, we are now due for a major shake-up. Samuel Bateman is correct. Nothing has been accomplished in the last sixteen years. We have no Medical Plan for the nation. Our infrastructure is crumbling as we speak. Our poor are increasing daily without any help. Our needy are ignored. Our veterans too are just ignored. Our legal system is in shambles as the corrupt lawyers, prosecutors, and judges join the One Percent Rich, at the expense of our Citizens. But our Politicians are looked after for life—yes, **for life!**

"Not anymore!!!

"No, this has to change! Yes, my fellow Americans, it is time for the Independents and Samuel Bateman to return this country back to its people, its citizens. As of today, the two-party system is hereby abolished. We need a Government that works.

"We thank Samuel Bateman for bringing all this corruption to the attention of the American People. Now let's all vote for the Independents and turn this country around to what it used to be, but with at least three Parties as a minimum. Thank you, Samuel.

God Bless America.

Furthermore, since the arrest of the Senator and the two House Representatives, please be advised that I have decided to help Samuel Bateman with his election campaign!

First, I have decided to issue some Presidential Directives to end some of the existing problems:

Directive 1

Effective immediately, all Lobbyists are hereby outlawed and banned from all government facilities permanently!

Directive 2

Effective immediately, each State, as of today, the date on this document, shall be responsible for all their existing inmates at their own correctional facilities. There will be no further compensation from the Federal Government. Each State shall provide suitable and humane facilities for all of its inmates at their own expense and to, I stress, acceptable American standards.

The sum paid out to the States, to the tune of $80 billion in the last fiscal year, will be directed to our crumbling infrastructure.

Directive 3

Effective immediately, all offshore accounts shall now remain offshore! Any funds transferred back to the States shall be taxed at a 65 percent. This percentage shall be reviewed by the new administration in due course. The One Percent Super Rich will pay their income tax, at applicable rates according to their income, just like all Americans are expected to do. There will be no special reduced rates for the wealthy!

Directive 4

Effective immediately, all salaries and compensation packages presently enjoyed by the active members of the Senate, the House of Representatives, and the Supreme Court are hereby cancelled. Lifetime compensation to previous/retired politicians is hereby withdrawn.

"Let's face it, folks, the Two-Party System of the American Government has proven to be totally ineffective as nothing of any sustenance has ever been accomplished, due to the endless bickering and fighting between the two parties. This has to end!

"Health care has become a joke, but as long as the Politicians were looked after by the best health care package available (only to politicians), what did they care if the rest of American citizens had no coverage! After all, they were all right!

"Thus, after sixteen years, nothing concrete has been accomplished, except that the Rich got richer, the Middle Class has been virtually eliminated, America is crumbling, and still no health care.

"Isn't it about time that funds be allocated to bring back America to its original self? The greed of the Politicians, the Super Rich, has escalated beyond belief. Corruption in Washington, DC, is totally out of control and needs to be brought back into line.

"It is now very clear that the enemy of the American people is, in fact, the American Politicians, Federal, State, the Courts, the Corrupt legal system, the uncontrollable Law Enforcement Officers who shoot to kill at every opportunity, knowing full well that there will be no retribution!

"No, not any longer! There has to be a change!"

*   *   *

Back in an undisclosed location, Samuel, Elizabeth, and Samuel's trusted friend, Robert

Hampton, watched the impromptu address by the disgusted President, and now they realized that they had achieved what they had been striving for—to open the eyes of the American public to the Corruption in Washington, DC.

The arrest of the Senator and the two House Representatives had turned the page!

Unexpectedly Samuel Bateman and his Party, along with Jake Taylor and Chris Canyon, were invited to an impromptu lunch with the existing President.

Part 4

The New America

Chapter 36

The Tsunami Election

The electoral wave had changed as the American people realized that a massive change was about to happen, as they anxiously waited for the Election Day.

Yes, the Tide had changed—it really was now a Tsunami! The sitting Democratic and Republican Senators and House Representatives were resigning so fast, and both Parties were having difficulties filling in the vacant slots. By the time the Election Day came, over half of the sitting Republican and Democratic Senators and House Representatives had resigned realized that they would be defeated by the Independents.

The Independents were becoming stronger by the day as the Election Day approached. Yes, all States now had Independent Candidates running for office; however, following the arrest of Republican Leader Senator Adams, numerous States were now lacking Democratic and Republican Candidates as so many, at the last minute had decided to withdraw their nomination just before the Election, knowing full well that their glory days were coming to an end and they didn't want to be part of a losing team.

Finally, on Election Day, the voting had the largest turnout ever as the Nation went to the polls; no one was denying access, and every American eligible to vote had turned out to cast their ballots.

And by an Executive Order issued by the incumbent President, all American citizens, including the inmates in all the Correctional Facilities across the Country, were, for the first time in history, permitted and encouraged to vote.

On Election Day, the entire Country and the World was on the edge of their seats! The tidal wave swept over the States. The Electoral Map that had typically divided the country into blue and red states was now virtually all white, the color selected for the Independents. There were some green for the Green Party and a few small red and a few blue spots showing up.

The nation was shocked yet delighted, and it celebrated. Perhaps now that the Country had eliminated the Fat Cats, the Average American would be heard again.

The existing President happily conceded defeat and wished the incoming President much success. He supported his revolutionary mandate and offered his personal assistance whenever needed.

Yes, the new President of America would be Samuel Bateman of the Independent Party.

The International Congratulations just poured into Samuel Bateman's office, the new President of the New United States. Yes, perhaps now the States could be United. Time would tell, but now it was definitely a possibility.

After the shocking results were tabulated, the Republican Party and the Democratic Party, were virtually wiped off the electoral map.

The Inaugural Ceremonies and Festivities were the largest ever recorded. All the Entertainers, Male and Female, in the Music and Entertainment industry out of Hollywood, New York, Nashville, all offered their services to entertain the massive crowds, and all for free.

There was a great absence of previous Presidents, Republican and Democratic Senators and House Representatives, and ex–Supreme Court Judges in attendance at the inaugural ceremonies, Samuel and his Independent Party Members, new Senators and House Representatives had an absolute field day. The Media across America was out in full force, and the media from around the world was all there as well as they wanted to witness the frenzy that was sweeping the country.

Yes, it was the beginning of a New Coming.

It was the Re-Birth of A Nation!!!!!!!

Chapter 37

The America of Old Returns

As soon as the new Members of the Senate and the House of Representatives were sworn in, the atmosphere in Washington, DC, changed completely.

Now there were no lobbyists to bribe the politicians and waste their time and no corporate executives wining and dining the Politicians. Now the Politicians had time to tackle the problems that faced the nation.

With the news that the Federal Compensation Package, to the tune of eighty billion dollars, was gone, suddenly there was a massive workforce available across the country. Inmates were being released in the thousands from the State Correctional Service Facilities to tackle the massive rebuilding of the country's infrastructure—roads, highways, bridges, railways, sea ports, airports, dams, electrical grids, etc.

Within weeks of taking office, the government had already sent groups of medical and economic specialists to Canada, Australia, England, and Sweden to investigate the national health plans in those countries.

In six months, President Bateman had promised America a new National Health Plan, that everyone in the fifty states and territories would be able to participate in, and at a reasonable rates.

If Canada, Australia, England, Sweden, etc., could make it work, then there was no excuse for not making it work, in America. Previously as all the Politicians already had a golden health plan for themselves, what did they care whether the rest of the population had one or not? They were looked after just fine. The health care plan was not a priority for any of them.

It certainly was a priority Now!

The final step was the creation of a committee to investigate the "George Bush Crash" that destroyed the middle class in America, made the Super Rich far richer, and why no one was ever held accountable for the massive destruction of the American people's lives and their hard-earned savings. In other countries around the world, national leaders have been held accountable for obvious corruption and convicted of national crimes, so why not in America?

The committee was to examine the extent of the involvement of George Bush, Dick Cheney, and others in the Crash, just who benefitted from it, and where the money went and to whom.

Yes, ex-President Bush and his Advisors would have a lot of explaining to do. It was not OVER!

Yes, a simple example was provided: An individual bought a two-week, two-bedroom, time-share condo in Kauai, Hawaii for $ 75,000. When the Bush crash hit two weeks later, that unit was valued at exactly $ 0, yet a $3,000 maintenance fee was still applicable yearly on that valueless property. Where did the $75,000 go? Who benefitted from it? Why was the loss never explained to the individual? Yes, this was simply one example of what happened.

House prices plummeted, the Owners lost fortunes—who benefitted? Again, there were no explanations! And so on. Answers were needed, required, and were pending. The entire Crash needed a clear explanation to the American Public, and if crimes had been committed, which they obviously had, then those accountable, now living like royalty, would be brought to justice, and if that included the President and the Vice President, so be it. Everyone in American was accountable—yes, even the President!

Yes, President Bateman had a mountain to climb, but this time he had people who were committed to, and interested in the country, they once knew, once called America!

Chapter 38

The End of an Era in Lexington

With the proposed Assassination of Samuel Bateman, per the senator's deal, the continual drug problems and the bust, and all the corruption in the Lexington area, the FBI head office had decided it was time to Raid the Baldwin Building and stamp out the virus that had infected the region for so long.

So it was precisely 9.00 in the morning that the six FBI Cruisers and the four army Jeeps pulled up at each side of the Baldwin Building; no one was going to escape. The army units secured the building as the FBI silently swarmed into the interior. The FBI was rounding up all the employees. Everyone was arrested!

Jake and Chris proceeded to Aldo's and Dwayne's offices, which were located on the second floor. Then without knocking on the door, Chris opened the door and burst in, his automatic in his hand. Aldo looked up and just about had a conniption.

"What the hell is this?"

"G'day, Aldo, so we meet again," said Chris with a sinister smile, as Chris directed Aldo back to his desk.

"I don't know you! Who the hell are you?" inquired the bewildered Aldo in desperation.

"Oh, Aldo, that's not true, my good friend. You definitely do. You know me all right, and you have for a long time! Just to refresh your memory. Remember, you're the one that always held me so that your sadistic boss, Dwayne, could punch me at will, and you were the one that tied me up so that Dwayne could whip me with his belt, so that I couldn't defend myself, first, back in Australia—yes, my back still bears those scars—yet you just stood there and laughed. You thought it was all really funny. Yes, and that was after you guys had killed the poor innocent and beautiful Olivia some years back, remember?"

"You remember Olivia? Yes, the beautiful lady who had made the mistake of marrying the phony heartless Dwayne, and you remember all the abuse she took from Dwayne? Then when she refused to play Dwayne at his stupid games, you two threw her into the crocodile-infested river back in Australia and laughed...yes, you remember that, don't you, Aldo? Don't you?"

Aldo stood there with a completely blank look on his face. He couldn't believe what was happening as these two supposedly FBI agents had burst into his office.

"Then once again, and that was after you guys killed my Mother and Father here in Lexington, on a deserted side road, again a few years ago, then you again held me so that Dwayne could beat me to a pulp, and then on the ground, you and Dwayne kicked the crap out of me before you pushed me into the muddy dirt ditch at the side of the deserted side road. That was all fun for you wasn't, Aldo? You and Dwayne were killing your-selves laughing all the while as I was close to death. Yes, I'm sure you remember. And as I said, that was that car bomb that I miraculously escaped. Yes, oh yes, I'm sure you remember that, Aldo. Don't tell me you don't remember how courageous you both were that night. You remember that all right!"

"Eric Baldwin? You are Eric Baldwin? I don't believe it! You are not him. He is dead! Besides, you look nothing like him!" rambled Aldo.

Chris laughed. "Yeah, you assumed he was dead. You and Dwayne wanted him dead, but isn't it amazing how one changes when one becomes a Navy SEAL?"

"You're a Navy SEAL?"

"Not quite, Aldo," responded Chris, shaking his head. "No, Aldo, I am a "Navy SEAL Operative." There is a slight difference."

"Dwayne made me do it. It was him all the time!" responded Aldo, now showing signs of the coward that he actually was.

"Sure, he did, but you enjoyed it too, and you never resisted doing it," responded Chris as he moved closer to Aldo, who was cowering backward until his back touched the wall.

"Ahhhhhh," uttered Aldo, now scared out of his mind.

"Well, today, Aldo, you have really reached the end of the road. Today everything is over for you, as now you are now heading for the county jail, where you are going to rot until you wither away to nothing, but then the other inmates may remember you too and choose to do something else, and not wait that long.

"So, Aldo, you see, I'm the Avenging Angel for our dear Olivia, my mother, Jesse, and my father, Wayne!" hissed Chris.

Unexpectedly Chris suddenly laced into Aldo with all his Navy SEAL expertise. Frankly Aldo was totally outclassed. He didn't stand a chance against Chris. In fact, he was actually useless. Chris expected some retaliation, some resistance, but Aldo was a phony too. He was incapable of providing any defense for himself against Chris's blows. The fact was Aldo could not fight. All along, he had always had the soldiers there to look after him. Chris pulverized him completely. He was bleeding all over, with various broken limbs and facial bones, almost whimpering. Two agents quickly came in and removed him.

"We'd better get him to a hospital for a little patchwork before we officially arrest him," advised

Jake to the two agents as they removed him from the room.

"Okay, Jake, we are down to the last man standing, aren't we?" Chris smiled. Jake just nodded his head, also smiling. He too had waited a long time for some form of revenge against Dwayne.

The door to Dwayne's office was still closed. Chris noticed that the door was hinged with really old hinges that still had removable pins, so with his knife, Chris silently removed the two pins. Then together Chris and Jake kicked the door off its hinges and sent it crashing to the floor.

Dwayne, wearing a pair of earphones and listening to some classical music, hadn't heard what was going on around him. He was totally oblivious to the FBI Raid.

"What the bloody hell is going on, Aldo!" screamed Dwayne as two strangers dressed as FBI agents entered his office, both holding automatic revolvers in their hands.

"Well, well, well…we met again, Uncle," said Chris in a matter-of-fact manner.

"'Uncle?' What do you mean 'Uncle'?" shouted Dwayne.

Then as Chris had Dwayne cornered in his office, they both stood facing each other, not moving. Suddenly Chris pulled off his shirt and turned his back to Dwayne. "Remember now, Uncle?"

"Eric? Can't be! But…but…you are dead," responded Dwayne, totally shocked. His flabby body began to shake with fear. This was a different Eric. He had killed his nephew.

"Yes, Uncle, I was almost dead, just the way you wanted me, my loving, considerate, and helpful Uncle. Yes, your one and only nephew that you beat the crap out of not once, but twice. Yes, once in Australia and once here again in Lexington on a deserted side road at night, and that was after you killed my Mother and Father with that car bomb, remember….but thanks to Fate, somehow I survived, which upset you to no end, so you were intent on finishing me off yourself, then as Aldo held me, you took it out on me again.

"But then Fate stepped in. Amazingly some people came to my rescue, and again I survived yet again.

"Yes, Eric Baldwin disappeared that night, but he didn't die! Like the legendary phoenix, Chris Canyon appeared to take his place!

"Then three years as a Navy SEAL Operative changed the scrawny, gangly kid into a powerful fighting machine. So, Uncle, it's my turn to take it out on you—whether you like it or not. You really do have it coming, you got that? This time there is no Aldo or any of your soldiers to hold me now. They are all headed to the hospital or the federal jail, where no one has been bought off.

"Dwayne, there is not going to be a third opportunity for you. This time it's my turn, and unlike you, I don't need anyone to hold you, and trust me, you are going nowhere, except to hell," said Chris commandingly without any fear or hesitation. This time, he was in charge, and this time, this fat slob was going to get what he deserved and what was coming to him.

Slowly Chris edged closer to Dwayne, who moved nervously backward, not knowing what to do or what to expect. Dwayne, just like Aldo, was a complete phoney, a coward, and he too couldn't fight his way out off a paper bag, so to speak, even if his life depended on it. This time it did!

"And don't even try to make a run for the door, Dwayne. You'll never make it, as today is also my turn to get even!" shouted Jake.

"You remember that young innocent brunette schoolgirl you raped and then killed? She just happened to be my fiancée. But your crooked, corrupt, and paid-for cronies in the Police Force and the County Courts got you off. That was then, but this is now!

"There is no one here now, to help you, Mr. Godfather, Baldwin. You got that, you scumbag? I have waited a long time for this, a long time to see you squirm, but this time there is only you. There is no help coming, you bastard. The day of judgement has finally arrived, and after today, we'll, that's Chris and I, we will be able to put the past behind us, as we will have exterminated a vile, venomous snake in the grass here in Lexington."

"Jake Sanders. You?" gasped Dwayne recognizing Jake again. Now Dwayne standing alone, without Aldo or any of his soldiers there to help him, was literally shaking in his shoes.

"Then you also killed your first wife, Olivia, and ran out on the law in Australia. We also know that you had Chris's parents killed, and as Eric didn't die in the car bomb you thought you had killed him for sure on a deserted country side road. Yes, you tried several times to kill him too. But he survived!'' elaborated Jake.

"You'll never pin that murder rap on me!'' shouted Dwayne defiantly.

"Oh, Dwayne,'' laughed Jake, "give us some credit. There is no pinning involved. Just listen to this tape as you confess to the murder of Jessie and Wayne Baldwin, your brother and his wife, and your disappointment that your nephew, Eric, wasn't killed in the same car bomb as you had hoped,'' said Jake nonchalantly as he clicked on his hand help tape recorder.

When Dwayne heard his own voice confessing to the murder, he just about had a bird!

Then surprisingly, Chris had had enough. He sprang into action as he took out his frustrations on the hapless Dwayne, who just like Aldo, crumbled from his onslaught. Dwayne, now on his knees, shaking from fear, was bleeding all over. His one arm was broken. His face was an absolute mess. His nose was broken, as was his cheekbone and numerous other bones in his body. Finally Jake held up his hand.

"Okay, Chris, now it's my turn.'' He raised his silenced automatic slowly up and pointed it at Dwayne's head.

"No, no, no!'' shouted Dwayne. "This is all a mistake!'' Dwayne pulled out his revolver, which he carried tucked into his belt on his back, and began to raise it toward Chris and Jake.

"Yes, Dwayne, it was all a mistake," repeated Jake as he squeezed the trigger and fired two quick shots into Dwayne's skull.

Both Chris and Jake took deep breaths as they looked at the bleeding, mangled body of Dwayne on the floor. Finally, in their own minds, they now both acknowledged that their long-awaited revenge was now complete.

Now they could return to their own private lives and put this episode out of their brains.

During the next several days, the FBI had found several of Aldo's soldiers who confirmed that Dwayne had also killed Alice and that she was now under a six-inch concrete slab in the city's new parking garage. Yes, Dwayne had shot Alice. This time the death was reported and not covered up. Four written statements from four Baldwin soldiers were provided confirming her death.

Thus, the Baldwin organization finally had closed its doors and was no longer operating, and the Taurus Corporation eliminated from the books. It was over. All pertinent files were taken by the FBI and microfilmed for their records. All other documents were shredded and destroyed.

The Taurus Corporation was erased from the Corporation Records, and the Baldwin name just disappeared. In the final scenario, the Baldwin House was demolished, and the people of Lexington were able to erase the memory of this corrupt and evil virus that festered there, in that old building, for so long.

The FBI had had just eliminate the Lexington virus, and the Community was grateful.

As Chris was the only remaining relative of the Baldwin family and Taurus Corporation Bank Accounts, Chris inherited a fortune.

Chris immediately created a charitable organization with the remaining funds and subsequently commissioned a new library and recreation/youth center to be built on the Baldwin site, dedicating it to the memory of Jessie, Olivia, and Wayne and donated it to the city of Lexington. The city was grateful, needless to say.

Even the new President of United States, Samuel Bateman, had volunteered to come and open the building as it really had been Chris's and Jake's discovery of the Politician's conspiracy to have Samuel assassinated that had really turned the tide in the federal election, and catapulted Samuel and his Independent Party to power in congress.

And so, the era of corruption came to a conclusive end.

America was reborn.

Part 5

The Return of the Nashville Rebel

Chapter 39

The Return of the Nashville Rebel

The call from Larry Fleming was totally unexpected, and a real surprise, needless to say, as Chris sat on a comfortable couch, his arms wrapped around Kiara, in his luxury condo over looking the luscious blue grass meadows of the famed Bluegrass Country Thoroughbred Estates disappearing into the horizon.

The call interrupted his passionate making-out activity with his glorious love, Kiara, his now wife. Yes, the love that they had shared before his Tour of Duty with the Navy SEALs and Kiara's time studying to become a doctor at the universities, was still burning bright.

Their three-year separation was now well behind them, as they moved forward with their love life. Their love for each other was still there, and it had just been revitalized as they had just reconnected again in their wild three-way reunion that included Kiara's vivacious loving mother, Alycia, and that the three of them had agreed to three years earlier. Yes, things were back to normal.

Chris and Kiara were One again, as Fate had determined a long time ago. They couldn't have been happier.

Unexpectedly the Phone rang!

Chris picked up the phone. "Hallo, Chris Canyon here."

"Hey, Chris, Larry Fleming. Remember me, and Kiara's graduation dance, where you entertained everyone with your fabulous songs, including Billy Fury's 'Once upon a Dream.'"

"Yeah, Larry, great to hear from you. Hey, how could I forget? It was a great night, and thanks for asking me to sing."

"Well, Chris, I didn't tell you, but I recorded your entire performance, and as I knew you had gone to join the Navy SEALs, Kiara told me, I held on to the tape, until now," advised Larry.

"No kidding?"

"Well, for your information, I've just presented your tape to RCA Victor Studios in Nashville and guess what, they were really impressed with your performance, and yes, they too all remembered the legendary Nashville Rebel from Lexington. Suddenly, after listening to your tapes, they were very interested.

"However, since the tape was three years old, and more importantly, they wanted to meet this Nashville Rebel in person, you have you come into their studios and record 'Once Upon a Dream' for the US market, as Chris Canyon, the legendary Nashville Rebel."

"Are you serious?"

"Absolutely, my friend, look we have to prove that the legendary Nashville Rebel is still alive and kicking! I know you still have a great fan base in the Lexington region, and I know the Nashville Rebel is a legendary figure in the South, so all we need to do is prove to them that you are still here and that you still have that amazing voice and can still sing and play that rocking guitar!

"Well Chris, you also have an additional advantage. You remember Jackie Shannon, your ex-social Director, in your High School? Well, she is one of the Directors at the Recording Studio now. I'm sure you remember her and her Young Girls Social Club."

"Yeah, I certainly remember her and her organization of young ladies. It was a real education How could I forget that!" Chris laughed.

"Regretfully, however, you have to remember, you never cut any Records when you were doing all the rounds, but in this region of Kentucky, the Nashville Rebel was a very well-known celebrity, a real legend. And don't forget you really wowed them at Kiara's graduation dance.

" Oh yeah. It was amazing, but they all knew you. So all we have to do is convince the studio that 'The Legendary Nashville Rebel' actually still exists and still has what it takes to excite the crowds," continued Larry.

"Anyway, listen, my friend, I've set up a session at the RCA Studio in Nashville next Tuesday, so you and I can fly in on Monday Night, record all day Tuesday, and then see what happens."

"What do you say?"

"Hey, Larry, what can I say? Let's give it a try."

"Great, Chris, I'll pick you up on Monday afternoon. The tickets are already arranged, and then we'll fly to Nashville for our sessions on Tuesday. Bring your guitar."

"Okay, Larry, see you on Monday."

When Kiara heard about this session up in Nashville, she was really excited.

"Oh my God, this is really great, Chris! Everyone will love the new Nashville Rebel. Just like I always have from that first day when we held each other's hands, and I'll never forget my graduation dance when the mysterious Nashville Rebel appeared from out of nowhere and really wowed everyone. It was so sensational, and the way you let the world know you loved me. That night was so special to me."

Chris just smiled. He was excited as well. After all his music really was his life, and now he had his second chance.

"I love you Babe, Kiara."

"And I love you too, Chris, and you know I always will!"

Chris smiled.

...........'Cause I got things to do and
Things to say, in my own way.........

The Nashville Rebel
had returned to the South!

The End